ST. NECTARIOS OF AEGINA

Ἀπολυτίκιον.

Ἦχος α΄. Τῆς ἐρήμου πολίτης.

Σηλυβρίας τὸν γόνον καὶ Αἰγίνης τὸν ἔφορον, τὸν ἐσχάτοις χρόνοις φανέντα, ἀρετῆς φίλον γνήσιον. Νεκτάριον τιμήσωμεν πιστοί, ὡς ἔνθεον θεράποντα Χριστοῦ· ἀναβλύζει γὰρ ἰάσεις παντοδαπάς, τοῖς εὐλαβῶς κραυγάζουσι· δόξα τῷ Σὲ δοξάσαντι Χριστῷ, δόξα τῷ Σὲ θαυματώσαντι, δόξα τῷ ἐνεργοῦντι διὰ Σοῦ, πᾶσιν ἰάματα.

Κοντάκιον.

Ἦχος πλ. δ΄. Τῇ Ὑπερμάχῳ.

Ὀρθοδοξίας τὸν ἀστέρα τὸν νεόφωτον
Καὶ Ἐκκλησίας τὸ νεόδμητον προτείχισμα
Ἀνυμνήσωμεν καρδίας ἐν εὐφροσύνῃ.
Δοξασθεὶς γὰρ ἐνεργείᾳ τῇ τοῦ Πνεύματος
Ἀναβλύζει ἰαμάτων χάριν ἄφθονον
Τοῖς κραυγάζουσι, χαίροις Πάτερ Νεκτάριε.

Μεγαλυνάριον.

Τὸν τῆς εὐσεβείας νέον πυρσόν, καὶ τῆς Ἐκκλησίας τόν φωστῆρα τὸν φαεινόν, τὸν θερμὸν προστάτην, καὶ ἔφορον Αἰγίνης, Νεκτάριον τὸν θεῖον, ὕμνοις τιμήσωμεν.

ὁ ἅγιος ΝΕΚΤΑ ΡΙΟ ς

ST. NECTARIOS OF AEGINA

MODERN ORTHODOX SAINTS

7

ST. NECTARIOS
OF AEGINA

Metropolitan of Pentapolis, great Theologian, Philosopher, Moralist, Educator, Ascetic, Mystic, Miracle-Worker and Healer. An account of his Life, Character, Message and Miracles, together with a Comprehensive List of his Writings, Selections from them, and an Essay on his teaching on God.

By

CONSTANTINE CAVARNOS

Institute for Byzantine
and Modern Greek Studies
115 Gilbert Road
Belmont, Massachusetts 02178
U.S.A.

PREFACE

This book is a product of persistent effort, which began twenty years ago, to become fully acquainted with the life, character, and thought of St. Nectarios of Aegina. It is the first book on this Saint to appear in English, or in any language other than the Greek.

More than a dozen books on St. Nectarios have appeared in Greek. These works, with few exceptions, possess real merit, both with respect to form and to content. However, they tend to be simply biographical and laudatory, and to concern themselves one-sidedly with his miracles. Not much is said about his publications, their contents, the important teaching they contain on many subjects. In this volume, I seek to give an account, not only to St. Nectarios' life and of some of his miracles, but also of the nature and scope of the more than thirty books and the many pamphlets and articles which he published. In addition, I present an extensive anthology from them on diverse topics, and an essay — based on six of his books — in which I summarize his remarkable teaching on God.

All parts of the present book appear in print for the first time, except for the eloquent "Life of St. Nectarios" by Archimandrite Joachim Spetsieris, and the "Miracles of the Saint" that follow. The Life and four of the seven Miracles, which I translated from the original Greek, were first published in the periodical *The Orthodox Word*, Vol. 2, No. 2 (April-May-June, 1966). In preparing these texts for inclusion in this book, I went over them carefully and made certain corrections and improvements in expression.

In the long "Introductory," I cite the most important dates and events in the Saint's life, note his main traits of character, and call attention to his holy way of life and to the manifold and widespread influence which he has exerted. Further, I devote considerable space to a discussion of his publications, speaking of each of them in chronological order.

The list of "Works of the Saint" is the most complete, systematic, and up to date one.

"On God" is a lecture which I delivered at St. Nectarios Greek Orthodox Church in Roslindale of Boston, Massachusetts, on November 7, 1979.

"Selected Passages from the Works of the Saint," pertaining to a wide variety of topics, have been culled from sixteen works of St. Nectarios, and have been translated for the first time.

As in the case of the other volumes of this series, I have included, as the frontispiece, a photograph of an icon done in the Byzantine style. This one, depicting St. Nectarios, was done in 1966 at Athens, through the hand of Vasilios Lepouras.

CONSTANTINE CAVARNOS

June, 1981

CONTENTS

ix

INTRODUCTORY

The divine Nectarios of Aegina, who after Sts. Cosmas Aitolos and Nicodemos the Hagiorite is the most widely known Greek Orthodox Saint, was born on October 1, 1846, in Silyvria, Thrace. At Holy Baptism he was named Anastasios. His parents, Demos and Balou (popular for Vasiliki) Kephalas, were simple, pious Christians. They brought him up in a manner pleasing to God, and did what their very limited means allowed for his formal education.

Having completed elementary school at Silyvria, he left his native place, at the age of fourteen, and went to Constantinople to secure employment and continue his education. At Constantinople, he found employment at a store and was able to earn a meagre living. In his free hours, he studied the writings of Orthodox

Church Fathers and ancient Greek writers. Also, he attended regularly church services.

Young Anastasios' desire to transmit edifying knowledge, developed rather precociously, led him at this time to begin making a collection of wise sayings, culled from his readings. Each day he made some of these maxims available to the customers of the store where he worked. He did this by writing them on the cigarette paper bags of Constantinople's tobacco sellers.

Anastasios next secured employment at the Dependency (*Metochion*) of the All-Holy Sepulchre in Constantinople. He was appointed an overseer of the children at the school of this Dependency and a teacher of the lower grades. This position enabled him to continue his studies by attending the higher grades. Thus began to be fulfilled his intense desire for higher education with a view to becoming eventually a theologian.

In 1866, at the age of twenty, he went to the island of Chios, in all likelihood at the advice and incitement of someone at Constantinople. Here he was appointed teacher at the village of Lithion. True to his character, which impelled him to seek to benefit so far as possible all his fellow men, he did not limit himself to his formal duties as a teacher, but sought also to edify and help all the villagers.

After a period of seven years as a school teacher at Lithion, he entered Nea Moni, an eleventh century Chian monastery that is famous for its Byzantine mosaics. In this, he was prompted both by his strong love of the monastic life, and also by his aspiration to further his theological learning. His love for the monastic life was kindled by a venerable Elder named Pachomios. This monk dwelt at the Skete of the Holy Fathers on the Provation Mountain of Chios. He is known as the author of the book *Defense of the Truth and Victory over the Devil*,[1] which has gone through three editions. In a letter to the disciples of Father Pachomios at the Skete of the Holy Fathers on November 1, 1905, on the occasion of the death of their Elder, Nectarios, then Director of the Rizarios Ecclesiastical School, calls Pachomios his "friend and guide in the arena of the spiritual way of life."[2] And in a letter written on the same day and addressed to the nun Xeni, Abbess of Holy Trinity Convent which he established in Aegina, he says: "Father Pachomios has died, and

I request you to write him in the diptychs; perhaps the blessed Elder expects this of you, because he was my guide at the beginning of my life
of spiritual endeavor."[3]

On November 7, 1876, after three years as a
novice at Nea Moni, Anastasios was tonsured a
monk, and his name was changed to Lazaros. A
year after his tonsure, he was ordained Deacon
by Metropolitan Gregory of Chios, and was renamed Nectarios. The same year, probably at the
exhortation of his mentor, Elder Pachomios, and
with the financial support of Ioannes Horemis, a
wealthy Chiot, he went to Athens to continue his
formal education.

In connection with Father Pachomios' role
here, the following passage from chapter 11 of his
"Catechetical Discourse," contained in his *Defense of the Truth and Victory over the Devil,* is
especially pertinent: "All the great Fathers and
Teachers of the Church were extremely well educated. Uniting external (secular) with internal
(spiritual) and divine learning, they saved the
Church from the many heresies that endangered
it. With their wise writings, they strengthened
Orthodoxy."

At Athens, Deacon Nectarios completed his high school studies. Having received the diploma, at the exhortation of his Chiot benefactor he left for Alexandria. There he explained his situation to Patriarch Sophronios IV. Seeing great promise in him as a servant of the Church, the Patriarch took him under his custody. At Sophronios' recommendation, he returned to Athens and enrolled as a student at the School of Theology of the University of Athens. Nectarios received for this the permission of the fathers of Nea Moni and the Metropolitan of Chios.

He enrolled in 1882, and received the Licentiate of the School of Theology in 1885. An excellent student, he held during this period a scholarship that was awarded to him after competition.

During his last year as a student of theology, he made his appearance as an author, publishing in pamphlet form some sermons which he had delivered. One of them is entitled *Concerning Faith*; another, *Concerning Confession*; and a third, *Concerning the Divine Eucharist*.[4] The thought in all is well-organized and set forth in a

clear, simple and concise manner, and with the
warmth that comes from the heart of one who
possesses authentic piety.

In the pamphlet *Concerning Faith*,[5] the Saint
undertakes to establish the nature and truth of
the Christian faith, drawing chiefly from the New
Testament. Although he believes that the evidence from Scripture is sufficient to prove the
truth of the faith, he also offers a rational proof
of the Divine origin of the teaching which constitutes the content of the Christian faith. The
sermon *Concerning Confession*[6] touches upon all
the essential points of the subject. St. Nectarios
makes extensive use of Holy Scripture. In addition, he uses insights pertinent to the value of confession contained in the writings of ancient Greek
writers, in particular Hesiod, Plato, and Plutarch.
Concerning the Divine Eucharist extols the importance of this Mysterion, calling it "the highest
of the Mysteria ('Sacraments') and the most necessary for man."[7] The text is divided into two parts.
In the first, he shows (a) the greatness of the Mysterion and (b) why we should partake of it. In the
second, he explains (a) how one should prepare
for it, (b) the benefits one derives from it when he
receives it worthily, and (c) how one should conduct oneself after receiving it. The treatment of

the subject in all three pamphlets is thoroughly Orthodox, illuminating, and convincing.

After graduating from the School of Theology of the University of Athens, the holy Deacon left for Alexandria. There he was ordained Presbyter by Patriarch Sophronios IV. The ordination took place on March 23, 1886, in the Patriarchal Church of St. Savvas.

In August of the same year he received the title of Great Archimandrite of the Patriarchal throne of Alexandria, in the Patriarchal Church of St. Nicholas at Cairo. At once there were committed to him the duties of Preacher and Secretary of the Patriarchate, and soon after those of the Patriarchal Epitropos[8] in Cairo.

St. Nectarios showed quite extraordinary energy and efficiency in the exercise of all these duties. Seeing his zeal and achievements, Patriarch Sophronios sought to widen the Saint's sphere of activity. Thus, on January 15, 1889, he ordained him Metropolitan of Pentapolis.[9] The ordination took place in the Church of St. Nicholas at Cairo. This Church it may be noted, was in a shabby state when the holy Nectarios was appointed Patriarchal Epitropos. Soon, with the generous help of his flock, he transformed it, through extensive iconographic decoration and other means, into a resplendent house of the Lord.[10]

As a Metropolitan, he was greatly admired and loved by his flock for his virtues, the exemplary Christian way in which he lived and fulfilled his duties as a churchman. This admiration and love aroused the envy of the clerics about the Patriarch, who aspired after the offices that had been given to our Saint, and even after the throne of the Patriarch, who was advanced in age. In order to have him removed from the Orthodox Church of Egypt, they sought to arouse the hatred of the Patriarch against him. To this end, they told the Patriarch that he aspired after the Patriarchal throne, and that he was guilty of insubordination and immorality. They thus succeeded in changing Sophronios' high opinion for the holy Father and causing his permanent removal from the Church of Egypt and return to Greece. At first, he was removed as Director of the Patriarchal office at Cairo and as Patriarchal Epitropos. His removal took place on May 3, 1890. Two months later, on July 11, he was dismissed by the Patriarch altogether from the Church of Egypt. The popular Metropolitan was sent away from Egypt without a trial, without explanation, and without being given an opportunity to defend himself.[11]

Something should be said here about his publications while in Egypt. In 1885, the year of his arrival in Egypt, he published a book entitled *Ten Sermons on the Great Lent*.[12] This appeared in Alexandria, when he was still only a deacon. His first book, "it testifies to his divine zeal and presages the future distinguished churchman and saint."[13] These sermons are clear and concise in expression, most moving and edifying, and show at once wide learning and great piety.

Two years later, after he had received the office of Archmandrite, he published at Cairo a pamphlet entitled *Two Sermons*.[14] This contains a sermon "Concerning Faith," and one "Concerning God's Revelation in the World." The first was delivered on the Sunday of Orthodoxy in the Patriarchal Church of St. Nicholas; the second, on an unspecified occasion, in the Patriarchal Church of St. Savvas. Although the subject of the first of these sermons is the same as that contained in a pamphlet which he published in 1885 at Athens, the treatment is different, the material new. It takes the form of a commentary on Hebrews,

chapter 11, verses 24-27: "By faith Moses, when
he was come to years, refused to be called the son
of Pharaoh's daughter; choosing rather to suffer
affliction with the people of God, than to enjoy
the pleasures of sin for a season; esteeming the
reproach of Christ greater riches than the treasures in Egypt: for he had respect unto the recompense of the reward." Taking this as his point of
departure, St. Nectarios undertakes to show that:
"(a) We ought to order our actions with reference
to our Faith. (b) We ought to prefer the afflictions
that go with the promise of salvation to the life of
luxury. (c) The believer ought to regard the reproach of Christ more precious than earthly treasures. (d) We ought to believe in recompense."[15]
To establish these points, he makes special reference to the Church Fathers. Thus, he remarks
that "our Fathers had a similar Faith, similar
principles, convictions and spirit."[16]

In the second sermon, he defends the reality of
miracles, as one of the ways in which God reveals
Himself to man in nature. The denial of miracles,
he says, implies the negation of Divine revelation,
which is the foremost doctrine of Christianity.
Basic in his defense is his distinction between two
worlds: the natural world and the spiritual world,

each of which has its own laws and operations. Our Saint incidentally touches upon other ways in which God reveals Himself to man.

As in his earlier publications, his treatment of the topics is fully in the Orthodox tradition, masterly, persuasive.

In 1888, our Saint published his second book, entitled *Concerning the Holy Synods, and Especially Concerning the Importance of the First Two Oecumenical Synods.*[17] This was printed in Alexandria. It is dedicated to the Patriarch of Alexandria Sophronios, whom he calls his protector and benefactor. In the Preface he notes that he was prompted to write this work by the charge, which he had recently heard, that the holy Synods were responsible for the decline and fall of the Byzantine State. He wrote this monograph, he says, to prove the opposite, that the Synods were important and necessary, and caused great benefit to the Nation and the Church. In order to demontrate this, he undertakes to give the whole history of the Seven Oecumenical Synods, and their precise character, without attempting to exhaust the subject.

A year after the appearance of the book *Con-*

cerning the Holy Synods, St. Nectarios published,
again in Alexandria, a pamphlet entitled *Address
Delivered at the Achillopoulion School for Girls
on the Feast of the Three Hierarchs.*[18] This address evidences the holy Father's great admiration
for the Three Hierarchs: Sts. Basil, Gregory of
Nazianzus, and John Chrysostom. He retained his
admiration for them throughout his life. They are
by far the most frequently quoted Church Fathers
in his two-volume *Treasury of Sacred and Philosophical Sayings,* which appeared between 1895
and 1896, in *Know Thyself,* which was published
in 1904, and other works.

In 1890, the year of his removal from the
Church of Egypt and departure for Greece, he
published in Alexandria another work, the second edition of the book *Sketch Concerning Religious Tolerance* by Eugenios Voulgaris (1716-
1806), one of the foremost Greek theologians and
educators of the eighteenth century. The first edition appeared in 1768. In a two and a half page
note which he appended at the end of Voulgaris'
text, St. Nectarios states that the text was reprinted with the greatest fidelity. Besides this
note, he contributed eighteen pages of notes taken
from a French work which Voulgaris used as a

basis for his treatment of the subject. He selected some of the notes contained in the French work, translated them and appended them in order to help the readers understand in a more precise manner certain parts of Voulgaris' work. This publication, particularly the note which St. Nectarios himself wrote and appended to the text, is of considerable value for understanding his critical attitude towards the Papacy, and his high regard for Voulgaris' work. He speaks of it as "a brilliant treatise on religious tolerance,"[20] and "a most truthful defense of the true religion of the Christian Greeks."[21]

Later, the Saint published in Alexandria two other books, written by another very eminent Greek educator, Neophytos Vamvas (1770-1855): *Christian Ethics*[22] and *Natural Theology*.[23] These appeared in 1893, three years after his departure from Egypt. Regarding these two works, he says: "Having found the *Natural Theology* and the *Christian Ethics* of the Blessed Vamvas at Cairo in the hands of a certain woman, we purchased them and printed them in Alexandria, and sent the manuscripts to the library of the Gymnasion of Chios."[24] Evidently, our Saint prepared the text of these works for publication while he was in

Egypt and gave it to the printer at Alexandria
before he left for Greece.

When he arrived in Greece, at Athens, he
thought of going from there to the Holy Mountain of Athos, to settle there and lead the life of
a monk. For he had a strong inclination for the
monastic life, having led it earlier for a number
of years at Nea Moni in Chios, as we have already
seen. He probably preferred to go to the Holy
Mountain than to Chios because the libraries
there far surpass those in Chios, and because
Athos has been the greatest center of Orthodox
spirituality during the last ten centuries. That the
first consideration must have been important for
him we can judge from his already manifested
activities as a religious writer. And that the second must likewise have been important cannot be
doubted, in view of his constant aspiration for the
highest spiritual attainments, testified by his writings. But many persons prevailed upon him to
stay in the world, so that he might greatly benefit
people through his preaching and personal
counsel.

Having sought employment as a Preacher, he
was appointed Preacher in the prefecture of Eu-

boia, one of the largest Greek islands, which lies
north of Athens. The appointment was made on
February 15, 1891. The holy Father served there
as a Preacher for two and a half years. His sermons, being very eloquent, full of wisdom and
warmth, and expressive of deep piety, won the
admiration of his congregations and effected a real
transformation in them. He succeeded in doing
for his Christian brethren, through his preaching,
what St. Cosmas Aitolos had done for his more
than a century earlier.

An example of the sermons he delivered during
that period is contained in his booklet: *Concerning the Results of True and Pseudo Education,*
which was published in 1894 at Athens.[25] This
work is divided into three parts: "I, Sermon: The
Call of Adolescents in Society; II, Speech: On
Exercise; and III, Writing: On Suicide." The
first was delivered on November 8, 1893, at the
Gymnasion of the city of Lamia, which is in the
Greek mainland west of Euboia. It is an exhortation to virtue, stressing the importance of culti-
vating the virtues of piety, love of truth, moral
wisdom, understanding, self-control, temperance,
justice. Our Saint draws here not only from the
Eastern Church Fathers, but also from the an-

cient Greeks, especially Plato and Aristotle. The other two parts of this booklet, although not sermons, are written in the same style as the first, and could well have been used as sermons. In the second, he looks at physical exercise from the ethical standpoint, as an essential part of developing the total human being, in whom the body, being healthy and strong, can serve as a good instrument of the soul. In the third part, he discusses the factors that dispose persons to commit suicide, the means of preventing or curbing suicide, and the Church's refusal to bury suicides.

While Preacher at Euboia, the blessed Metropolitan published four books: *Concerning God's Revelation in the World*,[26] *Holy Memorial Services*,[27] *The Oecumenical Synods of the Church of Christ*,[28] and *Sketch Concerning Man*.[29] The first of these is a full discussion of a subject he had already dealt with in his pamphlet *Two Sermons*, which was mentioned earlier. There, he devoted to it but 15 pages; in this book, 170. The latter is divided into three parts. In Part I, he deals with miracles and shows that these are not logically impossible and are not opposed to right reason. In Part II, he deals with this subject more extensively and, proceeding dialectically, concludes that

God reveals Himself in the world. In Part III, he shows the revelation of God in the world through the prophecies contained in the Old Testament. At the end, he appends an Epilogue, in which the revelation of God in the world is proved from the New Testament.

Holy Memorial Services is divided into four parts. In Part I, our Saint gives six arguments for the immortality of the human soul. These he regards as powerful and irrefragable. They are: (1) from the idea which we have of the immortality of the soul; (2) from the aspiration after the supreme good; (3) from man's idea of eternity; (4) from the love of the beautiful, the good, and the true; (5) from conscience; and (6) from the internal revelation of God. In Part II, he presents the teaching of the Orthodox Church concerning memorial services, and criticizes the errors of the heterodox Churches — the Roman Catholic and the Protestant. In Part III, he discusses the value of memorial services, citing particularly the testimony of the Canons of the Apostles, the writings of the Fathers of the Church, and the Liturgies and Diptychs of the ancient Church. In the last part he presents the eschatology of the Orthodox Church, and criticizes and rejects the Roman Catholic doc-

trine of a Purgatory as "erroneous, quite unaccept-
able, and without any foundation."[30]

*The Oecumenical Synods of the Church of
Christ* is a revised and enlarged edition of the already mentioned book *Concerning the Holy Synods, and Especially Concerning the First Two
Oecumenical Synods.*

Sketch Concerning Man "may be regarded as
the first Christian anthropology in the modern
Greek language."[31] In the Preface, St. Nectarios
explains that the writing of this book was occasioned by a discussion which he had with some col-
lege students that "the soul of man differs only in
degree from the soul of animals." To refute their
erroneous view, he says, he wrote and published
a small study, of only 16 pages, entitled *Concerning the Relation of the Human Soul to that of
the Animal and Their Difference.*[32] As that work
was too brief to treat the subject adequately and
to convince the students, he proceeded to write
this book of 233 pages. Its purpose is to show
what man is, and the chasm that separates man
from the animal. In the closing section of the
book (pp. 191-229), our Saint gives eleven proofs
of the immortality of the soul. Included among
these are the six proofs contained in his book

Holy Memorial Services. The first two of the latter appear unaltered, the third, fourth and fifth in expanded form, and the sixth revised. The five new arguments are: (1) from the holy life; (2) from the worship of God; (3) from knowledge; (4) from the social life of man; and (5) from the destiny of nations and divine Providence.

This book shows considerable acquaintance with the views of nineteenth century European scientists, including those of Lamarck and Darwin, of which he is particularly critical. Speaking of the evolutionists who trace the origin of man to the apes, St. Nectarios says, characteristically: "The followers of pithecogeny [the derivation of man from the apes] are ignorant of man and of his lofty destiny, because they have denied him his soul and Divine revelation. They have rejected the Spirit, and the Spirit has abandoned them. They withdrew from God, and God withdrew from them; for, thinking that they were wise, they became fools. . . . If they acted with knowledge, they would not have lowered themselves so much, nor would they have taken pride in tracing the origin of the human race to the most shameless of animals. Rightly did the Prophet say of them: 'Man, while in honor did not understand, but joined the beasts and became like them'."[33]

On August 19, 1893, the divine Nectarios was transferred to the Prefecture of Phthiotis and Phokis, part of the Greek mainland west of Athens. He served as Preacher there with the same effectiveness and fruitfulness that he had served in Euboia, until the time — some months later — when he was appointed head of the Rizarios Ecclesiastical School at Athens. During this period, he continued his activities as an author, and in February of 1894 he had ready for the printer a book entitled *Concerning Care of the Soul*.[34] This is made up of eleven homilies and sermons. The first four of these constitute a study about moral freedom. He seeks to prove that man possesses the power of free choice and self-control (*autexousion*), and hence is responsible for his sinful acts. In the fifth homily he discusses sin and shows that it is a great evil, and that we ought to repent. In the next two homilies he discusses Repentance, while in the eighth and ninth he speaks of Confession. The last two chapters, which he calls sermons, are concerned with the Divine Eucharist.

While stressing man's possession of the power of free choice and self-control, as part of God's image in him, St. Nectarios also emphasizes the need of utilizing this power for our liberation from bondage to the passions and vices, and for the acquisition of the virtues. He points out the need of Divine grace for full and enduring success in this endeavor, for our sanctification (*apopneumatosis*),[35] deification (*theopoiesis*).[36] "Man must work together with the Savior for his own salvation."[37]

On March 8, 1894, he was appointed Director of the Rizarios Ecclesiastical School by the Ministry of Church Affairs. He was to serve as Director of this School for a period of fifteen years: until December, 1908. This position gave great scope to the talents of our Saint as an educator. He not only directed the School most wisely, but also taught there various subjects and in addition preached.

His work as an educator here has been praised highly by Chrysostomos Papadopoulos, who succeeded him as Director of the School, and later became Archbishop of Athens. According to Papadopoulos, before St. Nectarios, the Rizarios School was in a state of great disorder. The administration was bad, the standards of conduct, ecclesiastical life, and scholarship were low. When he took over, he soon "brought about internal peace to the School, restored completely the ecclesiastical character within it, made special efforts for the ecclesiastical and moral training of the students, succeeded in bringing about a smooth, orderly internal administration of the School."[38]

St. Nectarios has also been praised highly for his work as Director at the Rizarios by his pupils who distinguished themselves in their chosen fields — for example Panayotis Bratsiotis and Nikolaos Louvaris, who became professors at the School of Theology of the University of Athens, and Presbyter Angelos Nissiotis. Bratsiotis remarks: "He was an excellent Director of the Rizarios School. A man of enormous learning, of pure ecclesiastical and ascetic character, with Christian politeness, he succeeded chiefly through these qualities in gaining the esteem of all: of the administrators, the professors, and the students."[39] Louvaris brings to light the following pedagogical method of punishing students who misbehaved. Instead of punishing them, he punished himself by staying without food. This proved a most effective means of discipline; for the students, having high regard for their Director, felt very sorry, repented, and corrected themselves.[40] Presbyter Nissiotis says: "As Director, he followed the students in the manifestation of their religious zeal, being present in the church from the beginning of the service of the Orthros and the Vespers, and standing during the whole service not at the bishop's throne, but at an ordinary stall that was at the right choir. . . . Within the Rizarios School there shone his luminous personality with his smile, his humility, and his love. The families of the professors and the counselors, as well as some aristocratic families that lived near the Rizarios School, considered it a great boon to go up to his office after the Liturgy and receive his blessing."[41]

As an educator, the chief concern of the venerable Hierarch was to incite and guide youth to become good Christians. This is evident not only from the testimony of those who knew him, but also from what he says in his books, many of which, during the period he served as Director of the Rizarios School, were written especially for the students of the School. Thus, in the Preface of the first volume of his *Treasury of Sacred and Philosophical Sayings*, which was published the year after he became head of the School, he says: "The profession of the teacher has as its foremost end the ethical and religious development of the youth who are being educated."[42] To this end, he

employed above all the Holy Scriptures, the teachings of the Oecumenical Synods and the Eastern
Church Fathers. Next for him in importance were
the writers of classical Greek Antiquity: philosophers, poets, rhetoricians, historians — but especially the philosophers Socrates, Plato and Aristotle. Like Clement of Alexandria St. Basil the
Great, and St. John Damascene, he believed that
properly selected passages from the ancients *prepare* the mind for the understanding of the Holy
Scriptures, and thus are aids to Christian upbring-
ing. So impressed was he by countless sayings of
the ancient Greek philosophers, that he remarks in
the Preface of the second volume of *Treasury of
Sacred and Philosophical Sayings*, which appeared
in 1896: "Greek philosophy is the fundamental
beginning of true development and education; it
is the tutor (*paidagogos*) of man, a guide that
leads to piety."[43]

While Director of the Rizarios School, he
preached often at the chapel of the School and at
other churches of Athens and the nearby city of
Piraeus. It was a time when preaching was seldom
heard in Greek churches, and people listened with
eagerness. His sermons captivated his congregations. As one of his most authoritative biogra-

phers, Archimandrite (later Bishop) Titos Matthaiakis remarks, "his simple and guileless style, the goodness of his heart, his extreme humility, together with his great learning, made a deep impression. . . . It is no exaggeration to say that the strengthening of the religious feeling of the people in Greece during the closing decade of the last century and the first decade of the present century was due to a great extent to the inspired and full of deep faith sermons of Saint Nectarios. . . . Through his sermons, unbelievers and enemies of the Christian faith were transformed into ardent champions of it, slanderers and accusers were disarmed, the avaricious and uncharitable became generous to the poor."[44] He took a real, profound interest in the people of these cities, and sought through his sermons to awaken them spiritually, to instruct them in the true Faith, to promote their inner development.

The fifteen years during which he served as Director of the Rizarios Ecclesiastical School were not only his longest and most fruitful period as an educator, but also his most productive one as an author. He published during this period, besides the already mentioned two-volume *Treasury of Sacred and Philosophical Sayings*, sixteen other

books, and various articles, including an important *Study Concerning the Holy Icons*,[45] which
appeared in eleven installments in the religious
periodical *Anamorphosis,* and an article *Concerning Oath*,[46] which appeared in the periodical
Hieros Syndesmos.

Treasury of Sacred and Philosophical Sayings is
a 942-page work, containing 478 chapters which
present religious and ethical sayings. The Saint
remarks in the Preface of the first volume that he
thinks the book will be very useful for everybody
— priests, spiritual fathers, preachers, teachers,
parents — "because in it everyone easily finds
whatever he might desire for his instruction."[47]

Our Saint explains that "the matter is so orga-
nized that there is an inner connection amongst
the many chapters, a natural coherence of ideas,
and an orderly transition from chapter to
chapter."[48]

There was to be a third volume, but this was
never published, and is not listed by the Saint's
biographers among his unpublished works.

The sayings are taken from the Old and the
New Testaments, the writings of the Eastern

Church Fathers, those of many ancient Greek writers, of some modern Greek and ancient Latin authors. By far the most frequently quoted Father is St. John Chrysostom. Next come, in order, Sts. Basil the Great, Gregory Nazianzen, John Damascene, Gregory of Nyssa, Neilos the Ascetic, Isidore of Pelusium, Cyril of Alexandria, John Climacos, Maximos the Confessor, and many other Fathers. Of the ancient Greek philosophers, the one from whom our Saint draws most often is Plato. Next come, in order, Plutarch, Socrates, Aristotle, Epictetos, Pythagoras, and some others. Of other ancient Greek writers, the most frequently quoted are Xenophon, Isocrates, Euripides, Menander, Homer, Aesop, Demosthenes, Herodotos, Sophocles, Theognis, and Thucydides. Of modern Greek writers, by far the most frequently quoted one is the eminent educator, classical philologist and philosopher Neophytos Doukas (*c.* 1760-1845). Next come Eugenios Voulgaris and St. Nicodemos the Hagiorite. The high esteem of our Saint for Voulgaris is manifested not only by the inclusion in this work of a number of passages from his works, but also by the already mentioned fact that he published a second edition of Voulgaris' *Concerning Religious Tolerance*. It is further manifested by his inclusion in his *Theotokarion*

(Athens, 1905) of two odes composed by Voulgaris, and by his use of Voulgaris' translation in
his poetic version of a work entitled *Kekragarion*
(Athens, 1910), the original of which is attributed
to St. Augustine. The passages from Nicodemos
are very few, evidently because at this time Nectarios was not sufficiently acquainted with the
work of this Athonite Father. In some of his later
works, he expresses high regard for Nicodemos.
Thus, in his brief Introduction of his *Psalter of
the Prophet-King David*, which was published at
Athens in 1908, he refers to him four times, and
calls him "the most holy and most wise Nicodemos the Hagiorite."[49] And in the Introduction of
his *Christian Ethics of the Eastern Orthodox
Church*, he cites Nicodemos' *Chrestoetheia*, "Mor-
ality," as a handbook with a sound scholarly
approach.[50]

From the references given in the text and in the
Epilogue of Volume 2, it is evident that in com-
piling the *Treasury*, St. Nectarios drew both directly from the writings of the figures mentioned,
and from earlier compilations of this type. In the
Epilogue, he says that he had in view *Hierogra-
phikon Apanthisma* ("Anthology from Holy Scripture") by Neophytos Metaxas, *Melissa* ("The

Bee"), *Opsimathes* ("Late Learner"), and some others. Among the others must be included the *Philokalia* which was compiled by St. Macarios of Corinth. Nectarios had probably been introduced to it by his spiritual guide at Chios, Father Pachomios. The latter refers to it in sections 4 and 186 of his "Catechetical Discourse," which was mentioned earlier. Our Saint lists it after some passages of his *Treasury*. Further, many sayings in the *Treasury*, of mystics such as Sts. Neilos, Maximos the Confessor, and Gregory Palamas seem to have been culled from the *Philokalia*.

In 1896, besides Volume 2 of the *Treasury of Sacred and Philosophical Sayings*, there appeared a 52-page book entitled *Epic and Elegiac Maxims of Minor Greek Poets.*"[51] The subtitle of this work is: "Maxims of Theognis of Megara; Pythagoras' Golden Verses; Phokylides' Poem of Admonition; and Maxims of Others." Under the subtitle is the statement: "For the Use of Schools." The compiler's name does not appear on the title page, and there is no Preface to indicate the purpose which the book is intended to serve at schools. But from an examination of its contents, one may safely conclude that its primary aim is moral edification. As a book for classroom use, it would also be used as a text for instruction in the ancient Greek language, particularly its poetic idiom. The last ten pages contain verses "From Various Authors," some by the Pre-Socratic philosopher Xenophanes "On Perfection," and three fragments from another Pre-Socratic philosopher, Heracleitos, "On God."

A year after this book appeared in print, St. Nectarios published a *Handbook of Christian Ethics*.[52] In this work he presents the ethical teaching of the Orthodox Church in a clear, methodical, scholarly manner, with ample documentation. It was published after it received the official approval of the Holy Synod of the Church of Greece. A didactic book, it was written and published especially for the use of his students at the Rizarios School, where he taught this subject.

This book appeared in a second, greatly augmented edition in 1965, with the title *Christian Ethics of the Eastern Orthodox Church*.[53] The text of this edition was prepared by our Hierarch while he led a monastic life in Aegina. Its Preface was written in 1920, the year of his death. Here he explains that, wishing to render it a work to be read by Christians at large, he revised and augmented it with this end in view. A significant piece of information which he gives here is that he taught Christian Ethics at the Rizarios Ecclesiastical School for fourteen years.

Continuing his efforts to provide the students of the Rizarios School with helpful textbooks, he published in 1898 a book entitled *Course in Pastoral Theology*.[54] The subtitle makes plain the purpose of the book: "For the Use of the Students of the Rizarios Ecclesiastical School." From a remark which he makes at the beginning of the Introduction, it is plain that this, too, is a subject which he taught at the Rizarios School.

In this work, he discusses the qualifications of prospective priests and bishops, their duties, and so on. But it contains also much that is of broader interest, such as discussions on the nature and purpose of the Church, its relation to the State, the seven Mysteria, the place of reason and argumentation in theology, the value of encyclopedic and philosophic knowledge for the bishop. St. Nectarios sets very high standards — moral, intellectual, and spiritual — for clergymen, especially bishops, devoting more than a third of the book to this topic. He takes a stand against *misology*, the hatred of argument or reasoning for the establishment or defense of truth and the refutation of

error, and against those who despise learning.[55]
He holds that secular as well as religious learning
is valuable, and is especially needed by spiritual
leaders in our age. For "today the validity of the
sources of Christian teaching is attacked with all
the power of historical criticism and philosophical
training, Sacred Tradition is rejected, the authority and knowledge of the Holy Scriptures is assailed, and the very first principles of Christianity
and of every religion are combatted — e.g., the existence of a personal God, and even the difference between matter and spirit."[56] In order to win
the battle against these forces, remarks the holy
Hierarch, spiritual leaders have need of all the
wealth of theological, philosophical, and encyclopedic knowledge.

At the end of the book, there is an Appendix
that is divided into thirty sections, in which many
canons of the Orthodox Church are given and
commented on. Of greatest interest and significance are the introductory remarks of the Appendix, under the heading: "Concerning the Validity
of the Canons of the Church." Thus, our Saint
quotes approvingly the first canon of the Seventh
Oecumenical Synod, which says: "We gladly espouse the divine Canons, and uphold firmly their
whole mandate — the Canons that have been set

forth by the clarions of the Spirit, the all-praise-worthy Apostles, those of the six holy Oecumeni-cal Synods, those of the regional Synods, and those of our holy Fathers. . . . And those individuals whom they anathematize, we also anathematize; those whom they unfrock, we also unfrock; those whom they excommunicate, we also excommuni-cate; and those upon whom they impose penance, we likewise impose penance."[57]

A year after the *Course in Pastoral Theology*, in 1899, St. Nectarios published a *Sacred Cate-chism of the Eastern Orthodox Church*.[58] The na-ture of this work, which is in the form of ques-tions and answers, is well explained on the first page. Here, in answer to the question: "In what manner do we expound the teaching of Sacred Catechism?" he answers: "The teaching of Sacred Catechism we expound methodically with a view to the precise transmission of the truths of the Holy Scriptures and of Holy Tradition, and the clear understanding of them. For this purpose, the teaching of Sacred Catechism has been divided into three parts: (a) the dogmatic, (b) the ethical, and (c) the ritualistic. In the first, there are ex-pounded the doctrinal truths of the Holy Scrip-tures; in the second, the moral truths of the Holy

Scriptures; and in the third, the truths and the
Mysteria of the Church, those which it received
from Sacred Tradition and preserves as ordinances
of the Apostles and Divine commandments." An
example of the precision with which our Saint
expounds the Orthodox Faith is provided by his
definition of "dogma," which appears in a foot-
note on the same page: "A dogma is a teaching of
the faith that has been handed down to the Church
by the Holy Apostles, has been developed in her
through the inspiration of the Holy Spirit, and
has been authoritively defined by her."

The theologian Panayotis I. Bratsiotis, remarks
about *Sacred Catechism of the Eastern Orthodox Church*: "This most comprehensive book,
which is simultaneously a handbook of Dogmatics
and of Ethics, and contains other rich theological
matter, we ourselves had as an aid when we were
taught this subject in the third year of the Rizarios
School by that unforgettable teacher."[59]

In 1901, St. Nectarios published two new
books: *Christology*[60] and *Study Concerning the
Immortality of the Soul and Concerning Holy
Memorial Services*.[61] The first work, original in
form and weighty in contents, is divided into three

parts: I. Concerning the Divine Character and the Redemptive Work of our Savior Jesus Christ. II. Concerning God's Revelation in the World according to the Holy Scriptures. III. Concerning the Fulfillment of the Prophecies in the Person of the Lord. Like the other works of the Saint that have been discussed, it was written for the edification of his fellow Christians. "Our chief aim in writing the present Christology was," he says, "to strengthen the faith of Christians, so that they might become firm and immovable in the faith and might live in the present age prudently, justly and piously, . . . welcoming the blessed hope and manifestation of the glory of our great God and Savior Jesus Christ."[62]

The text of *Christology* from the beginning to page 217 is new. From page 218 to 310, the end, it has been taken from his own already discussed book *Concerning God's Revelation in the World,* pages 44-171.

Study Concerning the Immortality of the Soul and Concerning Holy Memorial Services is an improved and greatly augmented edition of his book *Holy Memorial Services,* which was published in 1892. The 112 pages of the first edition have been increased to 230 pages of larger format. He was

prompted to write this work, he says, "by the observed indifference of most persons towards their
most sacred duties relative to their reposed parents, brothers and sisters, owing to their ignorance
of the importance and necessity of the Church's
holy memorial services."[63] Memorial services are
important and necessary, because they benefit the
souls of the dead and those who perform them.
The latter are "richly rewarded by God for their
benevolent act for the dead, and for their prayers
to God for the salvation of their parents and
brothers or sisters, relatives and friends."[64]

Inasmuch as memorial services presuppose the
immortality of the soul, before undertaking to expound the teaching of the Orthodox Church regarding memorial services, St. Nectarios discusses
the question of the nature and origin of the human soul, and then offers proofs of its immortality.
This part of the book occupies pages 7 to 80. He
attaches extreme importance to the doctrine of the
immortality of the soul. It occupies a central place
in his teaching. We have already noted that at the
beginning of his book *Holy Memorial Services* he
gave six proofs of the immortality of the soul. In
his *Sketch Concerning Man*, which was published
the next year, he included these proofs and added

five new ones. He included these eleven proofs, in abbreviated form, in his *Sacred Catechism*.[65] In *Study Concerning the Immortality of the Soul* the number of proofs increases, as he seeks to establish in his readers a firm and unshakable belief in the immortality of the soul. He regards such belief as essential for taking holy memorial services with due seriousness, for striving for our perfection and salvation and that of others. He remarks characteristically in this connection that "if we view man as a purely material being, whose existence ends at the grave, then virtue and perfection are barren suffering and vain display. . . . Those who deny the immortality of the soul undermine both the moral law and the foundations of societies."[66] St. Nectarios' view in this matter is fully in accord with that of St. Gregory of Nyssa, who stresses the need of "a firm and unmovable belief in the soul's continuance." "Human life," says Gregory, "will be bereft of virtue, unless an undoubting confidence with regard to this be established within us. What, indeed, has virtue to stand upon in the case of those persons who conceive of this present life as the limit of their existence, and hope for nothing beyond?"[67]

The saint of Aegina gives twenty arguments for

the immortality of the human soul — the largest number that has been given by a Greek of any period or by an Orthodox Church Father. Some of these arguments are new, others are reformulations of proofs given by Plato, the Byzantines or later Greek writers. He brings in new insights, and argues in an original and vigorous manner.

The second part of the book contains, besides five chapters on holy memorial services, with much more material than is present in his earlier book on the subject, a 29-page Appendix on repentance and confession.

Continuing assiduously his literary activity, St. Nectarios published in 1903 a large, 583-page volume on the Gospels, entitled *The Gospel Story through the Harmony of the Texts of the Holy Evangelists Matthew, Mark, Luke and John*.[68] It is a work unique in the Greek language. In writing it, the holy Father had recourse to Constantin von Tischendorf's *Synopsis Evangelica*. This served him in the historical classification of the material of the four Gospels.[69] *The Gospel Story* was written not for specialists, but for "the edification of the faithful of the Church in general, and for those who study Sacred Letters."[70] It contains all the material of the four Gospels, presented in chron-

ological order. In this way, a unified story is
formed, in which there is narrated according to
the order of time all that is said in the texts of
the Evangelists Matthew, Mark, Luke and John
regarding the teaching and the deeds of Jesus
Christ.

St. Nectarios used *The Gospel Story* as a text-
book in his course on the Interpretation of the
Gospels that he taught to third year students of
the Rizarios School.[71]

In 1904, he published a *Book of Contrite
Prayers*.[72] This contains prayers and hymns for
every day of the week, taken from the *Great Horo-
logion* and other liturgical books of the Orthodox
Church. It includes, for instance, the Exapsalmos,
the Small Apodeipnon, Canons of Entreaty to the
Theotokos, the Anabathmoi in the eight modes of
Byzantine chant, Troparia chanted in celebrating
the memory of various Saints, Doxastika, Apoly-
tikia, and the Akolouthia of Divine Communion.

Book of Contrite Prayers appeared in 1913 in a
second edition, which was enlarged by the inclusion of the First Hour and the Canon of the
Akathistos Hymn.

The same year, our Metropolitan published five other books: *Know Thyself, or Religious and Ethical Studies*; *Study Concerning Repentance and Confession*; *Study Concerning the Mother of the Lord, the Most Holy Theotokos and Ever-virgin Mary*; *Study Concerning the Mysterion of the Divine Eucharist*; and *Study Concerning the Saints of God*. *Know Thyself*[73] is an Aretology, a work concerned with the virtues and the vices opposed to them. The virtues dealt with are: faith, hope, love, justice, truthfulness, the virtues of the cognitive part of the soul, those of the spirited part (the will and the emotional power), and those of the appetitive part. In treating these subjects, he draws from Holy Scripture, the Orthodox Fathers, especially John Chrysostom, Basil the Great, Gregory Nazianzen, Gregory of Nyssa and Cyril of Alexandria, and from the ancient Greeks, particularly Plato, Aristotle and Plutarch. At the end he appends a discourse on virginity in the form of a letter addressed to the Nun Eusebia. This discourse is an exaltation of virginity and the monastic life, and at the same time a work of spiritual counsel.

Significantly, the Preface of *Know Thyself*, in which the discourse on virginity appears, was written just one day before St. Nectarios went to Aegina — a small island not far from Piraeus — with a view to founding a monastery for nuns. On September 10, 1904, according to his biographer Archimandrite Joachim Spetsieris, our Saint went to Aegina for this purpose, accompanied by three nuns. The next day he found a suitable site, the destroyed monastery of Zoodochos Pighi. Thereupon he began taking the necessary steps to reconstruct it. He renamed it the Holy Trinity Convent.

The occasion for founding this Convent was provided by some pious women who used to go to him to confess and receive his counsel. They often expressed to him the desire to embrace the monastic life. Having established the Convent, he sent these women there. He entrusted their maintenance and care, and that of the three nuns who accompanied him to Aegina on September 10, to Archimandrite Theodosios Papaconstantinou. The latter, who was Abbot of a monastery in Aegina, used to send a priest of his monastery to officiate at the church of the Convent on Sundays and holy days. This continued until St. Nectarios retired from the Rizarios School in 1908 and withdrew to the Convent. During that period, he sent from time to time letters of counsel to the nuns. Thirty-five such letters have been published by the Athonite monk Theocletos Dionysiatis in his book *Saint Nectarios of Aegina, the Miracle-Worker.*[74]

Study Concerning Repentance and Confession is an enlarged and rearranged edition of the already mentioned Appendix with this title in *Study Concerning the Immortality of the Soul and Concerning Holy Memorial Services,* which appeared in 1901. The nature of Repentance and Confession is clearly explained, and their importance is duly emphasized.

Study Concerning the Mother of the Lord is another short treatise, numbering 31 pages. Our Saint defends here the Orthodox doctrine that the Theotokos "was a virgin before she gave birth (to Christ), was a virgin when she gave birth, and remained a virgin after she gave birth, keeping her virginity intact."[75] While calling attention to the exalted position she occupies in the Orthodox Church, he notes that Orthodoxy avoids the heresy, which appeared in the third century, of worshipping the Theotokos, giving her the honor appropriate only to God.[76] He discusses the various appellations that have been used in speaking of her, and closes the book with an encomium to the Theotokos and a note on the hymn to her that begins with the words "Truly it is Meet" (*Axion Esti*). Profusely documented, this treatise is intended especially for the learned who question the Orthodox view of the All-Holy Virgin Mary, especially the Protestants.

It will be recalled that St. Nectarios dealt with the subject of Holy Communion in a pamphlet which he published at Athens in 1885. In his *Study Concerning the Mysterion of the Divine Eucharist*,[77] which appeared in 1904, he treats of the subject in a much fuller way: the 16 pages of small format that constitute the pamphlet increased to 35 large pages. He incorporated, in their original form, all the contents of the pamphlet from page 6 to the end. These constitute pages 19 to 27 of the book. The rest of the text is new.

The emphasis which the divine Nectarios puts on Holy Communion is reminiscent of a similar emphasis that one sees in the writings of the Kollyvades, such as St. Macarios of Corinth and St. Nicodemos the Hagiorite. Like them, he deplores those who do not receive Holy Communion regu-

larly because of sheer indifference to the benefits
that one derives from it, and not because they are
hindered by some sin. He remarks that "whether
we receive Holy Communion unworthily, or we
avoid it, we have no life."[78] And he reminds us of
Christ's statement: "Except ye eat the flesh of the
Son of man, and drink His blood, ye have no life;"
and "Whoso eateth my flesh, and drinketh my
blood, hath eternal life, and I will raise him up at
the last day (John 6: 53-54)."[79]

It should be pointed out that the holy Hierarch
was at one with the Kollyvades also on the matter
of Memorial Services. The Kollyvades held that
Memorial Services should not be performed on
Sundays, but on Saturdays. He remarks: "The
holy Fathers did not ordain that Memorial Services be performed on Sunday, but on Saturday;
that is, not on the first day, that of the regeneration of man, but on the Seventh, that is, on the day
of his death. For the Seventh day of creation saw
the death of man. . . . Wherefore the divine Fathers most wisely ordained that Memorial Services
be performed on Saturday, that is, on the day of
death, and not on Sunday, the day of the Resurrection, which is a symbol of the resurrection of the
dead at the Second Coming of Christ."[80]

Like the three books just discussed, *Concerning the Saints of God* is a brief treatise. It comprises only 32 pages. But it is a work of extraordinary interest, for here one reads what a *Saint* says about Saints. The book is divided into two chapters. In Chapter I, St. Nectarios speaks of the honor that is given to Saints by the Church Militant, the Church on earth, by venerating their relics and icons, commemorating them annually in feasts, eulogizing their struggles and the deeds they performed for the glory of God, and erecting churches in honor of their name. It does so, he remarks, not because it regards Saints as gods, but because it views them as holy individuals and friends of God. In support of what he says, he quotes from Church Fathers such as Sts. Basil the Great, John Chrysostom and Gregory the Theologian, and various other ecclesiastical writers. In Chapter II, he speaks of the intercessions of the Saints as a dogma of the Church, and defends it by referring to many passages of the Old and the New Testaments and to Sacred Tradition. Also, he answers the Protestant objections to the honor given to Saints and to the belief in the intercessions of the Saints, by referring to the Holy Scriptures.

In 1905, St. Nectarios published his first book

of poetry, entitled *Theotokarion, or Small Book of Prayers.*[81] It is intended to serve as a handbook for those who want to express their love to the Theotokos and to honor her by reciting such hymns. Also, it was composed as an expression of personal gratitude to her. "Having been taught by our Universal (*Katholike*) and Apostolic Church that it is meet to bless the Theotokos and Ever-virgin Mary," says our Saint in the Preface, "I have composed some odes and hymns in praise of the All-Holy Mother of the Lord, who is quick to listen, help, and protect those who invoke her; and also as an expression of my infinite gratitude to her for her many benefactions to me."

The poetry of the *Theotokarion*, though designed to be chanted and not merely to be read, belongs to the category of religious poetry for personal use, rather than to that of liturgical hymnography for use in church. It utilizies rhyme, a feature that is alien to Orthodox liturgical poetry.

A second, greatly augmented, edition of this book was published in 1907, the number of pages being increased from 52 to 292. "The fervent desire to laud the Theotokos," he remarks in the Preface of the new edition, "prompted me to write new odes and new hymns. . . . 105 new odes were composed, 53 new hymns, and 9 canons." This edition has been reprinted twice in recent years: in 1967 and 1972, a fact which shows that it continues to stir the religious sentiments of the Greeks. It owes this power to its literary merits, the deep religious faith and the strong religious feelings which it expresses.

In 1906, our Hierarch published a book entitled *Pandect of the Divinely Inspired Holy Scriptures*,[82] written by Antiochos the Monk (7th century), of the Lavra (Monastery) of Saint Savvas in Palestine. He took the text from Migne's *Patrologia Graeca*. The *Pandect* contains 130 discourses in which, as Antiochos remarks, is "condensed the entire Holy Scripture, both the Old and the New (Testament), in such a way as neither to become a burden, nor to leave out any of the things that tend to help and to lead to the salvation of the soul."[83] In each chapter, the author deals with some ethical topic, and thus the work constitutes, in the words of St. Nectarios, "a beautiful system of moral theology, made up of sayings from the Holy Scriptures and the ancient teachers of the Church, whose names Antiochos seldom mentions."[84]

In preparing Migne's text for publication, the
blessed Father corrected it in many places, either
by using his own judgment, or by having recourse
to the Holy Scriptures or to the Church teachers
from whom Antiochos took the sayings. His purpose in publishing it was "the moral instruction
of the readers."[85] He addresses it to all pious
Christians.

A year after the appearance of the *Pandect*, he
published a *Priest's Manual*. This book is an
abridgment of his *Course in Pastoral Theology*,
and in part of a supplement to it. Chrysostomos
Papadopoulos, Archbishop of Athens, said the following about it: "The indefatigable writer of useful books, the Most Reverend Metropolitan of
Pentapolis Nectarios, through this treatise offers
a helpful resource to the clergy for the enrichment
of their knowledge. In the first chapter, he examines Priesthood as a sacred service, in compari-
son with that of the Old Testament, giving all the
pertinent details. Thus, he discusses the three orders of the Priesthood, the chief work of the
priest, and the succession of the Apostolic office.
He points out the distinction of the three orders,
against those who deny it, and the divine origin
of the Priesthood. In addition, he lists the quali-

fications of the priest. The second chapter is devoted to an examination of the 'primacy of the Apostle Peter according to the opinion of the theologians of the Roman Church.' He opposes, in a well-grounded manner, the ideas which have been summed up especially by the Constitutio dogmatica de Ecclesia Cristi of the notorious Council of 1870, which instituted the dogma of the infallibility of the Bishop of Rome. At the same time, he takes into consideration all the well-known arguments of the Latin theologians, and refutes them in a well-grounded manner."[86]

The last book that was published by our Saint while he was Director of the Rizarios Ecclesiastical School was *The Psalter of the Prophet-king David, Put into Verse in accordance with the Tonal Base, with Interpretative Notes.*[87] In writing this work, he made use of the text of the Alexandrian codex, and the text and interpretation of Zygadinos contained in Nicodemos the Hagiorite's edition, entitled *Interpretation of the 150 Psalms of the Prophet-king David.*[88] About Zygadinos' book and Nicodemos' version of it, he says: "Euthymios Zygadinos, who flourished about 1110 A.D., had recourse to all the interpreters (of the *Psalter*) prior to him. His interpretation was

translated into simpler Greek idiom by Nicodemos the Hagiorite. We had recourse to this translation, and took from it some of the prolego-
mena."[89]

In this volume, St. Nectarios gives to all the
psalms metrical form in accordance with the tonal
base. In addition, he interprets the text, either by
giving it clearer expression, or by adding brief
footnotes that explain the meaning of the verses.
Further, at the beginning of each psalm he gives
an explanation about its subject-matter. In his
translation, he retains the idiom of the Septuagint
Psalter, and departs from its only when such a departure is necessary for the sake of the meter or of
clarity. Besides such changes, he often reorders
words and expressions, and sometimes he renders
verses according to the Hebrew text.

St. Nectarios' version of the *Psalter* is not intended as a liturgical book. This is evident not
only from its small format, quite similar to that
of his *Theotokarion*, but also from the manner in
which the text is presented. In writing it, he had
as his aim "to make the psalms understandable to
all, . . . and at the same time delightful."[90]
About the value of reading or listening to the
psalms, he quotes the following statement of Nic-

odemos the Hagiorite: "A psalm is conversation with God, a coming of Angels, a banishment of Demons, a cheerful state of souls, a rest from the toils of the day, an expulsion of the fears of night. A psalm is an invincible weapon, an inviolable treasure, a most beautiful adornment of the soul."[91]

In December of 1908, at the age of sixty-two, the blessed Nectarios resigned as Director of the Rizarios School and withdrew to Holy Trinity Convent in Aegina. He lived at this Convent the rest of his life, that is, until the year 1920, "as a true monk and ascetic."[92] He served as the confessor and spiritual guide of the nuns, and in the early years as the priest of the Convent. Continuing his activities as a writer, he published during this period half a dozen books, and authored others which remain unpublished. In addition, he performed various chores, such as the cultivation and watering of the gardens of the Convent, and carrying stones for the construction of cells.

With regard to his serving as a confessor, Matthaiakis says: "He received not a few clergymen from Athens and Piraeus for confession. His reputation as a Spiritual Father spread everywhere. As a confessor, he combined austereness with leniency; where the circumstances required this, he provided the medicine of penance; he admonished and saved souls. Among other gifts, he had that of foretelling things that would happen to the faithful. Many of those who confessed to him relate what the Saint foretold them."[93]

As founder and director of Holy Trinity Convent, he aspired to render it an exemplary monastery in Greece, and its nuns models of virtue and perfection.[94] He spent all his savings for reconstructing the church of the Convent, building cells and other edifices. Instituting the strict monastic system, the coenobitic, he made the best qualified nun Abbess, and required strict observance of the rules of the sisterhood. In order to enlighten the nuns and novices as much as possible in matters of the Faith in general and of the monastic life in particular, he offered them instruction daily after the vespers. The number of nuns reached 33 in his lifetime. The Convent continued to thrive after his repose. Today, it is one of the most frequented places of pilgrimage in all of Greece.

In withdrawing to Aegina, St. Nectarios did not

become something he was not already, a monk. As Matthaiakis, remarks, "during the period (1894-1908) when he was Director of the Rizarios School, he led essentially a monastic life."[95] Earlier, he had led a strictly monastic life in Chios, as we have seen. At the Convent in Aegina, he was simply able to become more fully what he already was. Freed from the demanding duties of administrative work and teaching, he was now able to turn inwardly, to practice inner attention and mental prayer more continuously, more successfully. In his book *Know Thyself*, which was published in 1904, the year when he founded Holy Trinity Convent, he says: "The monastic way of life is self-denial and submission to the Divine law, non-possession of property, self-control, hardship, struggle with unceasing prayer for the achievement of virtue, and patient endeavor to attain perfection."[96] It was in order to lead just such a life to the fullest extent possible that he withdrew to the monastery.

The great mystics of the Church, the hesychasts, had a strong attraction for holy Nectarios. In his writings, particularly beginning with his *Treasury of Sacred and Philosophical Sayings*, one finds many references to them — for example to Sts. Macarios the Great, Mark the Ascetic, Neilos the Ascetic, Isaac the Syrian, John Climacos, Maximos the Confessor, Niketas Stethatos, Gregory Palamas, and Nicodemos the Hagiorite. Now he was able to lead fully the same way of life which they had led.

During his first year of monastic life in Aegina, he published his second original work of religious poetry, the *Triadikon, or Odes and Hymns to the Triune God.*[97] This small volume is somewhat reminiscent of the theological hymns of St. Symeon the New Theologian, a writer, incidentally, whom he does not seem to have studied. Their poetry is vibrant with Divine love. The odes and hymns are at once prayers to God, forms of praise of Him, and ways of exhorting his fellow men to lead a godly life.

Like the *Theotokarion,* this book is offered to pious Orthodox Christians as an aid in their private prayers.

Continuing his poetic activities, St. Nectarios went on to produce in 1910 a two-volume poetic version of a *Kekragarion* that has been attributed to St. Augustine.[98] The term *kekragarion* is employed by the Greek Orthodox to denote psalms

140, 141, 129 and 116, that are chanted at Vespers. It is derived from the opening words of the first of these psalms: *Kyrie ekekraxa pros Se*, "Unto Thee I have cried, O Lord," and is used as the title of this book because its contents are in the spirit of these psalms. The full title of this work is: *Kekragarion of the Divine and Holy Augustine, Bishop of Hippo, Put into Verse in accordance with the Tonal Base, following the Translation of Eugenios Voulgaris*. It is in small format, similar to that of the other, already discussed, poetic works of the holy Father. Like them, it is not presented as a liturgical book. Its contents are not designed to be chanted, but simply to be read for edification.

At the end of the second volume, on p. 262, St. Nectarios appends one of his own poetic creations, a beautiful and very moving "Hymn to Divine Love."

The *Kekragarion* was followed by a very important, original work of 566 pages, bearing this long title: *An Historical Study Concerning the Causes of the Schism, Concerning its Perpetuation, and Concerning the Possibility or Impossibility of the Union of the Two Churches, the Eastern and the*

Western.[99] It is in two volumes, of which the first appeared in 1911 and the second in 1912. The expenses for the publication of volume 1 were paid by the monk Panaretos, an iconographer of the Skete of Kafsokalyvia on Mount Athos. Panaretos wrote the dedication and contributed a Foreword extolling the book. He dedicates the volume "To Our Most Holy Lady Theotokos and Evervirgin Mary, the Mighty Protectress of the Holy Mountain of Athos and of all Orthodox Christians." His involvement in the publication is significant. It shows that St. Nectarios was in touch with the monks of the Holy Mountain, this great stronghold of Orthodoxy, and had the encouragement and material support of one of its hermits.

Our Saint remarks that this work may be called "a History of the Schism, because it was written on the basis of the historical events, with historical preciseness and impartiality." The purpose which he had in view "was the search for the truth and only the truth, and the proclamation of it for the defense of the rights of the Eastern Church. For clever lawyer-like theologians of the Western Church, who deal with this subject in a legalistic manner, attribute to the Eastern Church the causes of the Schism and the reasons for its perpetuation."[100]

The first volume covers the period from the time of the establishment of the Church to the death of St. Photios the Great. The second volume deals with the period from the death of Photios to the fall of Constantinople, that is, 1453. There was to be a third volume, which would cover the period from 1453 to the twentieth century. But this was never published.

In the Preface of the second volume, St. Nectarios indicates what occasioned the writing of this work. It was, "firstly, the publication of Papal encyclicals, through which the Eastern Orthodox Church was invited to recognize the primacy of the Pope and to become united with the Roman Catholic Church, in the sense of complete subjection to it. Secondly, it was the trampling on the rights of the Eastern Church, the counterfeiting of the truth, and the various insults that are being cast at her from time to time by fanatical Papists."[101]

His study of the causes of the Schism leads him to the following conclusions: "The most important causes are (a) the arrogant and anticanonical claims concerning the primacy of the Popes of Rome, which are opposed to the spirit of the one Holy Universal (*Katholike*) and Apostolic Church that is expressed in Holy Scripture and guarded by the seven Holy Oecumenical Synods; (b) the innovations that have been made, through which the Roman Church has gone away from the Orthodox Universal and Apostolic Church; and (c) the annulling of the validity of the Holy Synods, which alone are able to possess the truth of the Church."[102]

It was the Roman Church, concludes the holy Father, which "opened the chasm of separation, by changing the nature of the Church" through the institution of the primacy of the Pope. The separation "was completed at the time of Photios," who refused to recognize such primacy, "since the Church ran the danger of ceasing to be one Universal and Apostolic Church and becoming a Roman Church, or rather a Papal Church, no longer teaching the doctrines of the Holy Apostles, but teaching instead those of the Popes."[103]

With regard to the question of the possibility of the union of the two Churches, his study leads to this conclusion: "The conditions for the union

are such that they render the union impossible.
. . . Because each Church asks of the other nei-
ther more nor less than the negation of itself, the
negation of the fundamental principles on which
the whole structure of the Church rests. For the
Western Church is based on the primacy of the
Pope, while the Eastern Church rests on the
Oecumenical Synods. . . ."[104]

The next work of St. Nectarios is, like the one
just discussed, ecclesiological in nature. Its title
is: *Two Studies: I Concerning the One, Holy,
Catholic and Apostolic Church; II Concerning
Sacred Tradition.*[105] While his book on the Schism
deals with deviations of the Latin Church from
the one Catholic and Apostolic Church, i.e. from
the Orthodox Church, this deals with deviations
of the Protestants from the true Church. "The
present studies," he says, "were written for the
defense of the truth that is being attacked by the
Protestants, who reject unwritten Sacred Tradition and the visible Church of Christ, and accept
only the written teaching of Christ and the Apostles."[106] The book is addressed to Orthodox Christians, to protect them from the proselytizing activities of the Protestants, who "traverse sea and land
to make one proselyte."[107] We undertook, he says,

"to refute all their arguments, to criticize their errors and defend the truths which are being attacked."[108]

According to the Protestants, remarks St. Nectarios, "churches are superfluous, the functionaries of the Church are superfluous, superfluous are the Mysteria, the traditions, the interpreters of the Scriptures, those who purify and sanctify souls through confession and remission, superfluous also are offerings and memorial services for the reposed, and prayers of entreaty for the living, addressed to the Mother of the Lord and to the Saints for their intercession with God. . . . Also, they reject every external form of worship, deny the holiness and power of the precious cross, reject the veneration of holy icons and of holy relics and, generally speaking, reject all that our Church reveres and respects as holy and sacred."[109]

Our Saint notes that he wrote a good number of other studies for the same purpose, namely, to criticize the errors of the Protestants, to defend the truths and practices which are attacked by them, and thereby protect the Orthodox, prevent them from being led astray. He lists the following as works of this nature:

Concerning the Mysteria; *Concerning the Mother of the Lord*; *Concerning the Precious Cross*; *Concerning the Saints of God*; *Concerning the Holy Icons*; *Concerning Holy Relics*; *Concerning Holy Memorial Services*; *Concerning Beeswax and Oil as Offerings, and Concerning Incense*; *Concerning Fasts*; *Concerning the Dedication of Holy Virgins to God, and Concerning Monasteries and the Monastic Life.*[110]

A year after the appearance of *Two Studies*, in 1914, St. Nectarios published a small book entitled *Historical Study Concerning the Precious Cross.*[111] He wrote this at the request of the Metropolitan of Athens Theocletos, "for the refutation of the false opinions and views of men gone astray,"[112] and to make known to the members of the Greek Orthodox Church the historical truth regarding the appearance of the Precious Cross to St. Constantine the Great and later to his son Constantios, the finding of the Cross by St. Helen, the veneration of it, the Divine power which is present in the Cross, and the use of it as an instrument of salvation.

In treating the subject, he draws from Scripture, the canons of the Oecumenical Synods, the Church Fathers, especially John Chrysostom, John

Damascene and Gregory Palamas, and from other writers.

He published one more book during the final, strictly monastic stage of his life: *Studies Concerning the Divine Mysteria*.[113] Here, the new luminary of the Church discusses the Mysteria, known in English as "Sacraments." At the beginning, he deals briefly with them in a general manner, while in the rest of the book, which is divided into seven parts, he treats of each of them separately, at length.

The Mysteria are defined as "certain mystical rites (*mystikai teletai*) employed for the salvation of those who believe in Christ. Performed by priests, using externally perceptible signs, the Mysteria transmit mystically the gifts of the Holy Spirit." They were received "from our Savior Jesus Christ through His holy Disciples, the Apostles."[114] The Church attributes to the Mysteria three essential characteristics: (a) a Divine origin, (b) a visible or perceptible form, and (c) the transmission through them of Divine grace to the souls of the faithful."[115]

Seven Mysteria are discussed: Baptism, Chrismation, the Eucharist, Repentance and Confes-

sion, the Holy Orders, Marriage, and the Euche-
laion or "Prayer-oil." They are explained in this
order.

Our Saint incorporated in this treatise two
works that were published in 1904: *Study Concerning Repentance and Confession,* and *Study
Concerning the Mysterion of the Divine Eucharist.*
He incorporated the first in its entirety and the
second up to page 27, omitting the section "Concerning our Duties to the Holy Altar." These
make up 60 pages of the 132-page book. In his discussions throughout the book, he draws from Holy
Scripture, the Oecumenical Synods, the Apostolic
Fathers, the Apologists and subsequent Fathers,
such as Basil, Chrysostom, Gregory the Theologian, Dionysios the Areopagite, Theodore the
Studite, Photios and others, and from some modern Church writers, particularly Konstantinos
Oikonomos.

The last publication of the Saint that appeared
in his lifetime was an edifying article entitled
"Study Concerning the Church."[116] This bears the
date July 1, 1919, and was published in 1920, in
the Festive Volume celebrating the 75th anniversary (1844-1919) of the Rizarios School.

In addition to his published works, he left a good number of unpublished ones in Aegina, at Holy Trinity Convent. A few of them, such as the second, greatly augmented edition of his *Handbook of Christian Ethics*, entitled *Christian Ethics of the Eastern Orthodox Church*, and two articles, one entitled "The Divine Liturgy of the Holy and Glorious Apostle and Evangelist Mark,"[117] and the other, "An Historical Study Concerning the Ordained Fasts,"[118] have been edited by Matthaiakis and published in *Theologia*. It is to be hoped that the rest will appear in print in the near future.

The extent and character of the writings of St. Nectarios place him among the great educators, moralists, and religious philosophers of modern Greece, and among the holy Fathers and Teachers of the Orthodox Church. Bratsiotis, speaking about the theological publications of our Saint, observes that they often go beyond the confines of strict scholarly research, aim at edification, and "are the product of a very lively concern to benefit the people. . . ." He also remarks: "For our meager theological literature, his works show originality in the choice of topics, many of which he dealt with for the first time among us and for the most part has not found a continuer of the particular inquiry. Indeed, that blessed and holy Hierarch . . . became *a continuer of the Greek Patristic tradition worthy of imitation.*"[119] Another eminent theologian, the late Amilkas Alivizatos, who taught at the School of Theology of the University of Athens, says: *"The books and other writings of Saint Nectarios are very remarkable, and some of them at that time filled obvious gaps in our theological literature* — for example, his book on the Harmony of the Gospels, his Pastoral Theology, his Psalter, and many others."[120]

St. Nectarios died in the evening of November 8, 1920, following hospitalization at Athens for prostatitis. His body was brought to Holy Trinity Convent in Aegina, and was buried by a priestmonk named Savvas. The funeral was attended by multitudes of people who came from all parts of the island, from Athens and Piraeus.

Savvas, now known as St. Savvas the New of Kalymnos, had dwelt for many years at the Skete of St. Anne on the Holy Mountain of Athos, and then at the monastery of Hozeva, near Jerusalem. In 1919, he was invited by St. Nectarios to teach the nuns of his Convent iconography and Byzan-

tine chant, for he was an iconographer and was
proficient in Byzantine music. St. Savvas accepted
the invitation. He went to the Convent and stayed
there for six years.[121] In 1925, he withdrew to the
island of Kalymnos for greater solitude, because
the fame of Nectarios as a Saint and miracle-worker was bringing an ever-increasing number of pil-
grims to the Convent. This hieromonk reposed in
1948 in Kalymnos.

Some time after the death of the holy Hierarch,
quite convinced that he was a Saint, Savvas undertook to paint an icon of him. To this end, he
locked himself up in his cell, and lived in complete confinement for a period of forty days. On
the fortieth day he came out of his cell holding
an icon of St. Nectarios. He gave it to the Abbess
and instructed her to place it on the icon stand
(*proskynetarion*) of the church for veneration.
This icon was the first one depicting St. Nectarios.[122] The year when it was done is not given
by the biographer of St. Savvas. In view of the
fact that Savvas left Aegina in 1925, the icon must
have been painted sometime between 1920 and
1925.

Many persons regarded Nectarios as a Saint in
his lifetime, because of his purity of life, his vir-

tues, the nature of his publications, his gift of foreknowledge and the miracles he performed.[123] The recognition of him as a Saint spread rapidly after his repose. Within the first decade after it, two biographies of him were written recognizing him as such. In the first of these, written in 1921 by the Cretan monk Avimelech, we read: "Although he has not yet been officially recognized as a Saint by the Holy Church of Christ, nevertheless the character of his life, the facts, and the various miracles which he performed in his lifetime and after death, as well as the ineffable fragrance emitted by his relics, testify that he received special grace and sanctification from God."[124] The next biography, written by Archimandrite Joachim Spetsieris, appeared in 1929. In this biography, he is emphatically asserted to be a Saint.

In 1937, a third biography was published, in which Nectarios is asserted to be a Saint, a monastic one, an *Hosios*. It was written by Archimandrite Theodosios Papaconstantinou — the monk who helped him establish Holy Trinity Convent — and is contained in his book *Akolouthia and Miracles of our Father among Monastic Saints Nectarios*.[125]

In 1926, there was formed at Athens the "Or-

thodox Christian Society Saint Nectarios of Pentapolis," to engage in religious and philanthropic
activities. From 1945 to 1950 it celebrated the feast
of St. Nectarios at the Church of Zoodochos Pighi
in Athens, near Omonoia Square. In 1951, it received official recognition as a religious and philanthropic organization, and began holding services in honor of St. Nectarios at the Church of
St. Nicholas "Pefkakia" in Athens. The next year,
it laid the foundations of a new church at Holy
Trinity Convent, named after St. Nectarios.[126]

Thus, beginning with the twenties, there was a
growing open popular recognition of Nectarios as
a Saint.

Official recognition of him as a Saint, by the
Oecumenical Patriarchate at Constantinople, took
place on April 20, 1961.[127] This recognition seems
to have been hastened by the publication in 1955
of Archimandrite Titos Matthaiakis' book, *Saint
Nectarios Kephalas.* Matthaiakis' publication contains an account of Nectarios' life far surpassing
in comprehensiveness any that had appeared until
then, his correspondence, opinions about him by
many prominent persons, clergy and laymen, an
Akolouthia in honor of him and a Canon of Entreaty to him, written by the foremost contem-

porary hymnographer of the Orthodox Church, Father Gerasimos Mikragiannanitis of Mount Athos.

Attention is called in Matthaiakis' book, again and again, to Nectarios' saintly character: his striking virtues of *humility, meekness, simplicity, self-control, detachment from worldly things, charity.* Also, his *spiritual gifts* are duly emphasized: his gifts as a *preacher* and *confessor,* and those of *fore-knowledge* and *working miracles.* Further, his important contributions to the Church as a writer are noted, as is also his powerful beneficent influence on many prominent clergymen and educators, and on the Greek people at large.

Especially weighty in supporting the view that Nectarios attained sainthood must be considered the testimony of men of extraordinary spirituality, who knew him well personally. Among these were the following: Archimandrite Joachim Spetsieris, whose life of St. Nectarios I have included in this volume; Archimandrite Philotheos Zervakos, who was for many years Abbot of the Monastery of Longovarda in Paros and an itinerant confessor; Archimandrite Amphilochios Makris, who was a brother at the Monastery of St. John the Theo-

logian in Patmos, a confessor, and founder of the
Convent of St. Minas in Aegina; and the hymnographer Gerasimos Mikragiannanitis, who leads a
hermit's life on Athos. Spetsieris was first a pupil
and later a close personal friend of St. Nectarios;
Zervakos and Makris had the Saint as their confessor and spiritual guide. They all clearly and
emphatically state that they regard Nectarios as a
Saint.

Father Zervakos says: "The ever memorable
Nectarios had the gifts of foreknowledge and
prophecy, gifts which only Saints have. . . . God
bestows His gifts especially upon those who have
the three great virtues of humility, faith, and love.
These three virtues adorned the unforgettable
Nectarios and rendered him a Saint."[128] Father
Makris remarks: "I regarded the holy Nectarios,
Metropolitan of Pentapolis, as a living Saint, filled
with the pure Orthodox spirit. . . . He was a
man of prayer, and had only one thought, to create centers of prayer. He spoke of mental prayer,
because he cultivated in himself this higher form
of prayer."[129] The testimony of these Spiritual
Fathers appears in Matthaiakis' book. That of Father Gerasimos Micragiannanitis, which is in the
form of hymns, likewise appears in that book.

Thus, in the apolytikion, contained in the akolouthia which he wrote in honor of St. Nectarios, he says:

> "Let us honor the offspring of Silyvria and the guardian of Aegina, the true lover of virtue who hath appeared in recent times, Nectarios, as a divine servant of Christ, for he gusheth up cures of every sort to those who cry out: Glory to Christ Who hath glorified thee, glory to Him Who hath magnified thee, glory to Him Who through thee effecteth cures to all."

Among the eminent men of the academic world who had him as a teacher at the Rizarios School, and were deeply influenced by his exemplary character and way of life, were George A. Soteriou, Professor of Byzantine Archaeology at the University of Athens and Director of the Byzantine Museum, Nikolaos Louvaris, Professor of Theology and Philosophy at that university, Panayotis Bratsiotis, Professor of Theology at the same university, and Haralampos Gieros, Professor of Philosophy at the University of Thessaloniki. Two of these educators, Soteriou and Bratsiotis, express their very high esteem for him in Matthaiakis' book. Soteriou says: "Those of us who were fortunate to study at the holy Rizarios School, when it was under the Direction of the Metropolitan Nectarios, remember his kindly character and the fascination which the radiance of his personality exercised upon us. . . . He has justly been recognized as an *Hosios*, for his saintliness was manifest: he possessed self-mastery, was ascetic, compassionate, a true Saint."[130] Bratsiotis observes: "I had the good fortune of having been a student of the truly holy Hierarch Nectarios. . . . He combined in an excellent way not only contemplation (*theoria*) with active virtue (*praxis*), and Hellenic with Christian wisdom, but also warm love of learning with assiduous practice of holy inner quiet (*hesychia*) and askesis."[131]

Many other prominent persons express the conviction in the pages of Matthaiakis' book that Nectarios was a Saint.

Besides such testimony and other pertinent material contained in Matthaiakis' book, what probably contributed significantly to the official recognition of Nectarios as a Saint in 1961 was the fact, testified in the book, that at the removal of his relics from the grave on September 2, 1953, they gave out an ineffable fragrance."[132]

Following the official recognition of the holy Father as a Saint, icons depicting him were done by Photios Kontoglou, foremost Greek iconographer, his pupils Rallis Kopsidis and Vasilios Lepouras, and many other icon painters. These icons or copies of them are to be seen in thousands of churches in Greece and abroad. Further, many churches have been dedicated to him. At least a score of churches have been named after him in Greece: at Athens, Thebes, Euboia, Karditsa, Kozani, Serrai, Mount Athos, Aigion, Laconia, Kalamai, Crete, Lesvos, Chios, Samos, Hydra, Kephallenia. In America, five parish churches have been dedicated to him — at Boston, Palatine (Il.), Seattle, Covina, Toronto — and several side chapels.

The number of churches named after St. Nectarios far exceeds that of churches dedicated to any other modern Orthodox Saint. This is undoubtedly due to the enormous number of miracles which he has performed since his repose, especially since the removal of his relics in 1953, and has led to his being called "St. Nectarios the

Miracle-worker." The periodical *Hagia Marina,*
which is published at Athens, has given accounts
of about two thousand miracles, most of them
miraculous cures. It gives dates, places, names,
and addresses.

The widespread recognition of Nectarios as a
Saint of the Church, and the growing number of
miracles performed by him, have resulted in the
reprinting of many of his books, the great major-
ity of which had appeared in print but once. It
has also resulted in the publication of a good number of books about him, showing deep admiration
of his character, way of life, and gifts. Most note-
worthy among these are the following: *Nothing is
Incurable for Saint Nectarios,*[133] by Dem. Panagopoulos; *Saint Nectarios,*[134] by Archimandrite
Haralampos Vasilopoulos, former Abbot of the
Monastery of Petraki at Athens; *Saint Nectarios:
The Hierarch, the Scholar, the Ascetic,*[135] by the
monk Theodoretos of Mount Athos; and *Saint
Nectarios the Miracle-worker,*[136] by the monk
Theocletos Dionysiatis.

Being regarded as a Saint not only of Aegina,
but also of Chios, where he was tonsured a monk,
his life and akolouthia, written by Father Gerasi-

mos Micragiannanitis, have been included in the
1968 edition of the *New Chian Leimonarion*.[187]
This is a folio liturgical book, containing the lives
and services (*akolouthias*) in honor of Chian
Saints.

The memory of the holy Nectarios is celebrated
on the 9th of November. On that day, the cantors
in Greek Orthodox churches read this synaxarion:

"On the 9th day of the same month, the Com-
memoration of our Father among the Saints Nectarios, Metropolitan of Pentapolis in Egypt, the
miracle-worker and founder of Holy Trinity Convent in Aegina, who reposed as a holy man *(hosios)*
in the year 1920."

And they chant, besides the already quoted apolytikion and many other hymns, the following
kontakion:

> "Let us praise with hearty joy,
> The new luminary of Orthodoxy,
> And the newly built bulwark of the
> Church;
> For having been glorified by the Spirit,
> He gusheth up abundant grace of healing,
> To those who cry out: Rejoice, Father
> Nectarios."

THE LIFE OF ST. NECTARIOS

By Joachim Spetsieris,

His Student and Friend[1]

Neither years nor times are of any significance before immortal virtue. "Virtue does not perish, even when one dies, for it is not corporeal."[2] Virtue does not die, because, as the Apostle of the Gentiles Paul says, Christ its judge is always the same: "Jesus Christ is the same yesterday and today and forever."[3] A truthful witness of these statements is the ever memorable worker of virtue Nectarios, Metropolitan of Pentapolis. He rose like another bright star in these gloomy days, when the dense darkness of materialism seeks to overwhelm the world.

The indefatigable worker of virtue Nectarios is proved to be truly great, not only through the

miracles that he continues to perform even after
his death, but also through his divine virtues and
his admirable life, which was nothing else than a
continuous and unceasing working of virtue.

This blessed one was born in Silyvria, Eastern
Thrace, of devout parents, Demos and Vasiliki
Kephalas, on October 1, 1846, and at Holy Baptism was named Anastasios. From his early youth
it was evident what kind of person he was going
to become: sensible, prudent, meek, self-control-
led, obedient to his parents who, even though un-
lettered, were very pious and brought him up "in
the nurture and admonition of the Lord."[4] Not
only the parents of little Anastasios, but all his
relatives and neighbors as well, used to look at
him with admiration.

He disliked children's games and found pleasure in praying and memorizing Psalms and holy
sayings. And from childhood one fervid desire
consumed his heart: to become after long preparation a preacher of the Gospel, even though the
poverty of his parents did not permit this. Divine
Providence, however, had destined him to become a shepherd of men and a teacher, for it foreknew his future virtue. As the Apostle Paul says:

"Those whom He foreknew He also predestined."[5]

At the age of fourteen, he left his birthplace and went to Constantinople, where some relative of his engaged him as a clerk at his store. While in the midst of worldly distractions, he did not neglect prayer, church attendance on holy days, and reading, in private, sacred and instructive books. Whatever sayings and apothegms he considered beneficial to his neighbor he wrote on packages and wrappings, so that the customers of the store might read them and profit spiritually, as he himself remarks in the Preface of his book *Logion Thesaurisma,* "Treasury of Sayings." He says:

"The present work is a product of long and intense work, and grew out of the prematurely developed ardent desire to transmit useful knowledge. For at an early age I envied above all the work of the teacher, and I eagerly turned to it. This work, however, was far above my zeal, because of my inadequate preparation for it. But the desire was strong and persistent. In order to fulfill it, I had recourse to the treasures of our ancestors, these being handy and at my disposal, and I could hoard them. Thus the work began and a meagre collection of sayings, opinions, and apothegms was made. But the means of transmitting them was also difficult, owing to the lack of money. I thought I could utilize as publication sheets the cigarette paper bags of Constantinople's tobacco-sellers. The idea seemed to me a good one, and was almost at once put into practice. Each day I wrote on many of these 'sheets' various maxims from my collection, so that those who used them might out of curiosity read the statements and be instructed in what is wise and good. Such was the beginning of the present book and the longing out of which it grew."

Who can read this and not admire the Saint's great love for his neighbor? In the words of the Apostle Paul, he employs everything, he uses every device, in order to benefit his neighbor morally.

Not long afterward, his fervid desire for study began to be fulfilled. He left the store and found employment as an overseer of children at the school in the *Metochion*[6] of the All-Holy Sepulchre, where he performed with great zeal the service that had been entrusted to him. In addition, he taught the lower grades and attended the higher ones.

At the age of twenty-two, he left Constantinople and went to Chios, where he was appointed a teacher at the village of Lythion. He remained here for seven years, instructing not only the students, but also all the peasants, exhorting them to piety and virtue, and leading an exemplary godly life.

Being an ardent lover of the monastic life, he often visited the Monastery of the *Hagion Pateron,* the "Holy Fathers," and conversed about the ascetic life with the very holy founder of the monastery, Father Pachomios. As he aspired to the Angelic Habit of the monks, he entered Nea Moni, "the New Monastery," and was tonsured a monk,[7] receiving the new name of Lazaros. Here he was appointed secretary, and stayed for three years. A year after his tonsure, the Metropolitan of Chios, the ever-memorable Gregory, ordained him Deacon and renamed him Nectarios. He was ordained on January 15, 1877, the anniversary of his Baptism.

While at Nea Moni, he studied unceasingly Holy Scripture and the sacred writings of the holy Fathers. At the same time his heart was being consumed by the burning desire to study theology and become useful to his fellow Christians. And the more he studied, the more this desire for study increased in intensity, even though the material means for such study were always inadequate.

But God, who, as the Psalmist says, "does the will of those who fear Him,"[8] enlightened Ioannes Horemis, a wealthy Chiot, and he sent Nectarios to Athens to study at his expense. The joy of Nectarios was indescribable when he arrived at that city, where the great luminaries of the Church Gregory Nazianzen and Basil had studied. Rejoicing that his longing began to be fulfilled, blessing the all-holy name of the heavenly Father, and praying for his benefactor, he devoted himself to his studies with zeal and self-denial. He studied day and night, and knew no other roads but that to the school and that to the church on Sundays and holy days.

After receiving his high school diploma, at the exhortation of his patron Ioannes Horemis, he went to the Patriarch of Alexandria Sophronios. The latter took him under his protection and sent him to Athens to study theology at his expense and that of Horemis.[9]

In 1885, having finished his studies at the university and received the Licenciate in Theology, he returned to Alexandria. Here, Sophronios ordained him Presbyter and Confessor[10] and, not long after this,[11] Metropolitan of Pentapolis and his Vicar (*Epitropos*) in Cairo. The oil had now been placed in the lamp. Everyone looked at him with admiration and spoke of him with great reverence, saying: "Here is a worthy functionary of the Most High; here is a man fit for the Patriarchal throne of Alexandria." As time went by, the reputation of the holy Metropolitan of Pentapolis grew. But the enemy of good, the devil and his followers, sowed weeds, babbling that he desired the throne of Alexandria.[12] As a result, the holy Father was removed from the Church of Egypt on July 11, 1890. He left Egypt and came to Athens, with the intention of going from here to Mount Athos, to lead a monastic life. But many persons, among them the ever-memorable Bishop of Patras Damaskinos, urged him to stay in Greece,[13] where he might greatly benefit the people through his life according to Christ and through his preaching.

When Nectarios arrived at Athens, he had no money at all, inasmuch as whatever money he earned in Egypt he used to give away to the poor and spend for the publication of writings that would benefit Christian readers. His disregard for money was such that many used to say: "Money and the Metropolitan of Pentapolis are two contrary things." And though he lacked even his daily bread, he did not ask for anything from anyone, nor did he say that he was in want, but waited with confidence for Divine succor.

Inner as well as outer promptings finally led the holy Father to stay in the world and preach. He sought and accepted from the Ministry of Church Affairs an appointment as a preacher. Initially, he served as preacher in the prefecture of Euboia.[14] After two and a half years, he was transferred to the prefecture of Phthiotis and Phokis,[15] where he preached the word of God until 1894. At this time he was invited by the Ministry of Church Affairs to assume the direction of the Rizarios Ecclesiastical School.[16] I was then a third year student at this school. Here he taught pastoral theology and other subjects to the upper classes.

Before his appointment as Director, the Rizarios School was always in a state of disturbance. When he took over the direction of the school, he at once brought peace to it, and it began to function normally. For he treated the students and the staff of the school as a loving father, and hence everyone loved and greatly respected him, obeying his counsels and admonitions.

He often came to the Exarchate of the All-Holy Sepulchre, where I was a priest, and many times when he departed I accompanied him as far as the Rizarios School, and listened to him as he spoke in a hortatory manner. One day, as we were walking to the school, he said to me: "When a man comes to understand his destiny, and that he is a child of the heavenly Father, that is, of the Supreme Good, he looks with contempt at the goods of this world. It is true that the virtuous man endures temptations and humiliations in this world; but he rejoices deep within his heart, because he has his conscience at peace. The world hates and despises virtuous men, yet it envies them, for, as our ancestors used to say, virtue is admired even by the enemy."

Everywhere, one might say, wherever he happened to be, the holy Metropolitan of Pentapolis taught piety, faith in God, and love of one's neighbor, like a true disciple of the Lord.

He departed from Egypt, as we have said, but

he left the immortal memory of a saintly man.
And when in 1899 a new Patriarch of Alexandria
was to be elected, Patriarch Sophronios having
died, Nectarios was invited by many Greeks to go
to Egypt and declare his candidacy to the Patriarchal throne of Alexandria. He went there, but
left for Athens at once, because, although he had
many supporters there, he perceived that the
clergy of the throne of Alexandria were acting in
support of Photios, who, being a member of the
brotherhood of the All-Holy Sepulchre, was also
supported by Patriarch Damianos of Jerusalem.
Seeing this, as he always loved peace, the holy
Metropolitan of Pentapolis returned immediately
to his position at Athens. As he told me: "Listening to the entreaties of our fellow countrymen, I
went to Egypt, not to cause uneasiness and fac-
tions, but to bring peace and love."

The periodical *Anaplasis*[17] wrote at that time:
"The candidacy of the holy Metropolitan of Pentapolis is one of the weightiest, because he is
among the most distinguished, well-educated, fervent and impeccable Hierarchs the Eastern Orthodox Church has to show. He is a very productive writer, an indefatigable worker of the Spirit,
having as his food and pleasure the service of the

word of God and truth. He is free of avarice to
the extreme, a fiery lover of goodness, serene but
strong, meek yet firm, pure in life. He is modest,
decorous, dignified in appearance and bearing,
above pettiness and intrigues, above passion and
envy. He is truly a superior episcopal personality.
And the harmonious totality of his excellences
places him among the most select ones. If someone
abler than he should be preferred for the Patriarchal throne of Alexandria, no one will rejoice
more than he; if he should be chosen, modest as
he is, he will have only one ambition, how to
prove himself worthy of his mission in all humility" (*Anaplasis*, 9 September 1899).

This is what *Anaplasis* wrote. But God had destined him to stay near the capital of Greece, even
after his death,[18] and through his holiness to teach
piety and love for God and neighbor, and immortal virtue in general.

A great number of persons used to go to him to
listen to his counsels and to confess. And as certain pious women often expressed to him the desire to embrace the angelic life of nuns, he for a
long time entreated the Lord to deem him worthy
of founding a convent near Athens. And God,
Who, as Holy Scripture says, "does the will of

those that fear Him,[19] listened to his prayers and was well pleased that he should become the founder of the Convent of the Holy Trinity in Aegina, which was established as follows:

The Monastery of the Dormition of the Theotokos in Aegina had as its Abbot Archimandrite Theodosios Papaconstantinou. Saint Nectarios, then Director of the Rizarios School, invited him and made known to him his desire to build a monastery for nuns in Aegina, if God deigned it; and he asked him if a suitable place existed there. The Archimandrite replied that near Palaia Chora there were some ruins which, according to surviving traditions and testimonies, belonged to a monastery for nuns, of which there survived only a little chapel dedicated to the Zoodochos Pighi[30] and two old cells. On September 10, 1904, the holy Father went to Aegina accompanied by three nuns. He was received at the pier by Archimandrite Theodosios. The latter led him to the Metochion of the monastery of which he was the Abbot, and the next day they proceeded to the dissolved convent, which was inhabited by an old woman that lived by the alms of pious Christians.

During that whole night, the Metropolitan and

his company prayed to the Lord to help them rebuild the ruined convent, if this were His will.
The following day, he met with the mayor of
Aegina, Nicholas Pepas, and made known to him
his intention, that is, that he wanted to rebuild
the destroyed convent, and begged him to repair
the two surviving cells and to cede the lot to him
for the reconstruction. The mayor promised to
comply with his wishes. That same day the Saint
left for Athens, for, being the Director of the
Rizarios School, he could not be absent from it.
Archimandrite Theodosios undertook the maintenance of the nuns, whom the holy Metropolitan
had left at the old convent; and on Sundays as
well as on other holy days he used to send a priest
of his monastery to officiate in the Church of the
Zoodochos Pighi. This arrangement continued
until the Metropolitan settled there in 1908.[21]
That year, the Saint retired as Director of the
Rizarios School, established himself in Aegina,
and began erecting the convent with zeal and self-
denial.

Who can describe the indefatigable toils and
struggles of the holy Metropolitan of Pentapolis
for the reconstruction of the convent? Quite vigilant regarding the observance of the sacred forms
in the doxology, chant, orderliness, solemnity, and

in the angelic way of life and Christly conduct, he forbade everything that was improper and out of harmony with the monastic life, especially the free entrance of men into the convent, and instituted a fully coenobitic system.[22]

He himself served as the priest of the convent, preached quite regularly the word of God, counseled the nuns both as a group and individually; and in a word, like "a lamp on a stand,"[23] he guided all in the way of salvation. Despite the many cares of the convent,[24] he did not cease writing edifying books for Christians living in the world. He wrote not a few and published most of them.

His publications include the following: 1) *Sermons,* 2) *Diverse Discourses,* 3) *Concerning the Seven Oecumenical Synods,* 4) *Concerning the Mysteria,* 5) *Concerning God's Revelation,* 6) *Concerning Man,* 7) *Concerning Care of the Soul,* 8) *Concerning True and Pseudo Education,* 9) *Treasury of Sayings,* 10) *Christian Ethics,* 11) *Pastoral Theology,* 12) *Sacred Catechism,* 13) *Christology,* 14) *Concerning the Immortality of the Soul,* 15) *The Gospel Story,* 16) *Study Concerning Repentance,* 17) *Concerning Confession,* 18) *Concerning the Mysterion of the Divine Eu-*

charist, 19) *Concerning the Saints of God,* 20)
Prayer Book, 21) *Know Thyself,* 22) *Theotoka-*
rion, 23) *Pandect of the Divinely-inspired Scrip-*
tures, 24) *The Psalter in Verse,* 25) *Triadikon in*
Verse, 26) *Kekragarion of the Holy Augustine,*
27) *Study Concerning the Causes of the Schism,*
28) *Concerning the One Holy and Apostolic*
Church, 29) *Concerning Holy Tradition,* 30)
Concerning the Divine Mysteria, 31) *Historical*
Study Concerning the Precious Cross, 32) *Con-*
cerning the Ever-Virgin Theotokos, 33) *Concern-*
ing Memorial Services. These he published in
Cairo, Alexandria, and Athens. His unpublished
works are ten in number. All his writings evince
his profound learning and true love of God and
of neighbor.

After settling at the convent, he lived an altogether spiritual life, being always in a state of
divine contemplation, like Arsenios the Great and
the other Fathers who are called Wakeful (*Nep-*
tikoi). Thus, having once met Constantine Sak-
korraphos, a native of Lamia who was for many
years close to the holy Nectarios, I asked him how
the latter was; and he replied:

"What can I tell you, Father Joachim! After
he settled at the Convent in Aegina he became all

spirit; he became, I can say, completely spiritual-ized, and leads an altogether spiritual life." And this when he had the care of the Convent. He never neglected mental prayer: "Lord Jesus Christ, have mercy upon me,"[25] and led a wholly spiritual life. This is why an exceptional sweet-ness radiated from his serene countenance, show-ing a holiness of sanctification in the grace of the Holy Spirit.

He was venerable, meek, kindly, humble, ex-tremely compassionate and charitable. He carried on the good struggle until he was assailed by a serious disease, or rather until the time came for him to depart to Christ, after Whom he had as-pired, and receive the crown of righteousness.

For many months he suffered from prosta-titis,[26] experiencing severe pains and enduring them with exemplary fortitude, always thanking the heavenly Father and blessing His all-holy name. Despite the sharpness of the pains, he at first refused to submit to medical treatment. How-ever, as the sisters persisted in their entreaties, he finally yielded and was taken to the Aretaieion Hospital.[27] Here, after a period of fifty days, he surrendered his spirit to the Lord on November 8, 1920, at the age of seventy-four.

Some time after his repose, strangely a fragrance was emitted by his holy body, filling the room in which it lay and from which it was carried the next day to the chapel of the hospital, and then by automobile to the Church of the Holy Trinity at Piraeus. While it was in the church, many went and venerated it, and with amazement noted the fragrant fluid that drenched his hair and beard.

The same day it was brought to the town of Aegina, and from there, as a precious treasure, to his Convent, where it was buried with great solemnity.

After five months, the nuns, desiring to construct a marble tomb, opened his grave and removed the holy body, which was whole and intact in every respect, emitting an ineffable fragrance, and bearing all the signs of holiness. It remained in the Abbess' office until the construction of the tomb was completed.

Three years after the death of the Saint, the nuns opened the tomb and found the holy body, as before, incorrupt and giving off the same fragrance. When the Most Blessed Archbishop of Athens Chrysostomos with devout interest took the initiative and personally examined it, he ordered that the body be placed again in the grave and be removed from it at the end of seven years from the date of his repose. The nuns acted accordingly, and the body was henceforth regarded as a sanctified one.[28]

I, too, went to the Monastery of the ever-memorable, Most Holy Nectarios, together with Archimandrite Theosodios Papaconstantinou, because I had been hearing a great deal about the sacred body. Now I confess with absolute sincerity that when I approached the tomb to pray I smelled the fragrance of the holy body; and I was so moved, that I cried with all my soul and all my heart: "Truly, the Metropolitan of Pentapolis Nectarios has received from God the gift of sainthood, like the Saints of our Orthodox Faith!"

The ever-memorable one performed not a few miracles when he was living, and continues to work many after his death. We omit them for the sake of brevity and because, as Gregory the Theologian says in his funeral oration on Basil the Great, "miracles are for the unbelieving and not for believers. The marks of Saints are their life according to God and their divine conduct." But is not the fragrance emitted by the sacred body a most truthful piece of evidence of the sainthood of Nectarios, a very clear sign of the indwelling in him of the grace of Jesus Christ?[29]

Saint Nectarios attained to the same enviable level of sainthood as the great luminaries and Saints of our Church. He did not ascend upon pillars, nor did he withdraw to hermitages, nor did he contend with cruel persecutions and tragic tortures, like those great combatants of our holy religion, the Martyrs; but we can say that his whole life was nothing else than a continuous doxology to God, and a tireless effort and assiduous concern to benefit suffering society morally and religiously. He lived *in* the world, but was *not,* as the Savior says, *of* the world. He trod on the earth, yet conducted himself like a citizen of heaven. He had the form of a man, but lived like an angel. He was clothed with flesh, but was a strict keeper and guardian of chastity. He associated with various kinds of persons, but spoke as a spiritual man, alien to the present world. He was transported by sublime ideals and warmed by the aspiration for moral perfection; and hence he abided in a state of inner calm and blessedness. His was a peace-making holiness, inspired by evangelical virtue and meditation on the eternal Kingdom of God.

MIRACLES OF THE SAINT

One of the most remarkable things about St. Nectarios is the fact that he not only argued vigorously for the real occurrence of miracles, but he has also provided abundant empirical justification for belief in them. He performed a number of miracles during his lifetime, and has worked countless others since his repose. Miracles have been reported from all parts of Greece and also from England, Germany, Australia, Canada, the United States, and South Africa. One of the most remarkable records of these miracles is contained in the 7th edition of the book *Nothing is Incurable for Saint Nectarios,*[1] authored by the lay theologian Dem. Panagopoulos. It lists and describes 221 miracles. Another writer, the Athonite monk Theodoretos, remarks in his *Saint Nectarios*[2] that the miracles exceeded 600 by the end of 1968. Their number is continually growing, as is evident from the periodical *Hagia Marina,* which is published by Panagopoulos and reports present day miracles.

Most of the miracles are in the nature of miraculous cures. All sorts of diseases and states have been reported healed through St. Nectarios. Going over the just mentioned book of Panagopoulos, I have noted among others the following, which I list in alphabetical order: arthritis, asthma, boils, cancer of the brain, cancer of the breasts, cancer of the intestines, cancer of the joints, cancer of the lungs, cancer of the stomach, cancer of the uterus, deafness, diabetes, eczema, epilepsy, fractured vertebra, gallstones, heart diseases, hemorrhage, hemorrhagic apoplexy, hemorrhoids, hepatitis, kidney stones, meningitis, migraine, nephritis, neuroarthritis, otitis, palpitation, paralysis, Parkinson's disease, peritonitis, phlebitis, pleuresy, polio, prostatitis, psychosis, rheumatism, sciatica, scleroderma, spondylitis, stammering, sterility, stomach ulcer, tuberculosis.

A great number of these cases had been given up by medical men as incurable. The cures were effected by prayers to St. Nectarios, anointing the patient with oil taken from the sacred lamp (*kandeli*) that burns at his tomb at his Convent in Aegina, or by placing his icon near the patient. Medical men have witnessed many of these miraculous cures.

The following seven miracles have been taken from Panagopoulos' already mentioned *Nothing is Incurable for Saint Nectarios*.

1

During the last days of his life, the Saint was in the room for the incurables of the hospital, among many poor patients who were at the point of death. Beside his bed there was a patient who was paralyzed for years. As soon as the Saint gave up his spirit, a nurse of the hospital together with the nun who had accompanied the Saint began to prepare the holy body for transportation to Aegina, for burial. When they removed the old sweater of the Saint, they placed it for convenience on the bed of the paralytic, and continued preparing the body. Strangely, the paralytic patient at once became well and rose from his bed, praising the Lord. This was the first miracle after the repose of the Saint, through which God our Lord confirmed the sainthood of Nectarios.[3]

2

Among the other offerings that are to be seen at the holy monastery of the Saint in Aegina, each of which corresponds to a miracle, there is a chain, about a yard long, that has on it a note which says the following: "Having been tormented by an unclean spirit, I was cured by the help of Saint Nectarios on March 18, 1954. — Paraskevopoulos Ioannes of Patras."[4]

3

Mrs. Anna Ioannou Katsounaki, a resident of Piraeus, relates the following:

In 1949, I was operated on at the anticancer hospital "Saint Savvas," because I was suffering from cancer, and they removed my entire uterus. When the definite period of therapy was over, Dr. Papaconstantinou joyfully declared that I had now escaped from the danger of death. "Do not be afraid any longer," he said. However, if you should ever see blood, then realize that your end has arrived, because it is a sign that cancer has appeared somewhere again and has produced a new malignant spot."

Eight years passed since then, when in May, 1957, I felt pains and annoyances in my abdomen.

These resulted in the appearance of blood one evening, that is, of the sign which was notifying me of my end. I spent all that night sitting in my bed and crying inconsolably. In the morning, my sister Eleftheria and her husband Nicholas Mortzanos, returning from Aegina, where they spent the Easter holy days, dropped in my home. Although I wanted to conceal my misfortune, in order not to sadden them, my sister, seeing me in my pitiful state, insisted on learning what had happened to me. As she justly insisted, my husband had to reveal the truth.

My sister at once, displaying no fear, but with composure and confidence, which she drew from her faith in the miracle-worker Saint Nectarios, approached me and consoled me, saying: "Don't be afraid, my sister. You believe in God and accept the many miracles of Saint Nectarios, which we have seen in our family."

At this point, she took out a small bottle from her handbag, containing oil from the sacred lamp of Saint Nectarios, gave it to me, and said: "Take this and pray to the Saint to make you well. I shall pray, too. Daub your abdomen with this blessed oil of the Saint, and rest assured that in this way you shall become well."

I complied fully with her suggestion, prayed, sought the help of Saint Nectarios. And behold the miracle! From that hour my annoyances stopped, I felt well, and the flow of blood ceased. From then until today, when I am writing to you about my case, in the year 1962, I am perfectly free of the accursed disease. Blessed be the name of Saint Nectarios![5]

4

Mrs. Antonia Panteli Argyriadou, a midwife, of 19 Iakovou Koumi Street, Canea, Crete, relates this:

In June, 1959, an abscess appeared on my right foot, which necessitated my going to the clinic of the late Rosenberg, to be treated for a fortnight. As my condition did not improve, I had to leave for Athens and finally to enter the hospital "Pammakaristos." I suffered continuously from dreadful pains, and my therapy became especially difficult owing to the fact that I suffered from sugar diabetes. One thing the physicians did was to remove continually rotten pieces of flesh from my foot, without using unaesthetics. Finally, the doctors decided to amputate my foot in order to save me, as all who had treated me till then had advised.

On the eve when the operation was to be performed, I saw in a dream a woman dressed in
black, and she asked me: "Why are you weeping?"
I replied: "My foot hurts, and tomorrow they are
going to amputate it." "Do not be afraid," she re-
marked at once. "In Aegina there is a good physician, and I shall telephone him to come and see
you." She went at once to the telephone and called
him up. I asked her: "Will he come by sea or by
land?" "By sea," she replied. But she had not finished, and the physician arrived. "Here is the
physician, he has come," she told me.

I did not see him. He approached my bed, but
I heard only the knocks of his iron staff, because
he entered from the rear and I could not turn
back to see him, as they had my foot tied onto a
special metallic device, to prevent me from moving it. I tried to see him, but I saw only his hand
lifted towards the light, behind and above me,
holding a large, new aluminum pitcher, from
which a small part on one side was missing. Then
I said: "Doctor, that pitcher is beautiful, but why
is that little piece missing?" "It does not matter,"
he replied. "That will be repaired. It will be-

come beautiful like the rest of the pitcher. Nothing will show." And he vanished.

I woke up immediately, uneasy. It was two o'clock after midnight. One of the nurses was there. She saw me uneasy and asked me if I wanted anything. I asked for some water and told her about my dreams perplexed. She listened attentively and said: "Then the physician is Saint Nectarios of Aegina. Make a vow at once to go there as soon as you recover."

In the morning, my foot was going to be amputated, as it had been decided. At nine o'clock, Professor Makris arrived, accompanied by six interns, and asked the nurse to unbind my foot. As soon as my foot had been loosed, the doctor saw that it was in very good condition. Having ascertained this, to his surprise, he changed his mind and did not go ahead with the amputation. On the same day, September 1, 1959, he was to leave for a trip abroad and to return twenty days later.

Upon his return, he found me perfectly well. The flesh which the doctors had removed from my foot had been restored, and my whole condition did not justify my staying at the clinic any longer. After a few days, I left the clinic and gratefully headed at once for Aegina, together with my husband, in order to thank my savior physician, Saint Nectarios, who had truly restored miraculously the missing part of the symbolic pitcher of my dream, through the regeneration of the parts of the flesh that had been cut off my foot.

I now enjoy perfect health and am ever grateful to the Saint of God, the miracle-working doctor, Nectarios.[6]

5

Miss Catherine Drettaki, a resident of 13 Strategou Koutouli Street, Koukaki, Athens, gives the following account:

My father, Emmanuel Drettakis, suffered from kidney stones. On July 17, 1962, he had a crisis of the kidneys. He went to the physician Androulakis and was examined. The latter said that stones had been formed and his condition was critical. Every day his condition became worse, and at the advice of the same physician he entered the clinic "Timios Stavros" on July 26, 1962. As soon as he was admitted, they tested his blood and found that the urea had reached 1.95. They X-rayed his kid-

neys and found that they were swollen and thus
the flow of urine was blocked. The physician told
us that an operation had to be performed. It was
to be performed on July 28, but my father entreated the doctor to postpone the operation, and
he postponed it to July 30.

The afternoon before the operation, my father
begged my mother to bring him some oil of Saint
Nectarios. As soon as she brought it, he got up,
prayed for five minutes, and drank it. The same
evening, I had a photograph of the Saint, which I
placed on my pillow, and I prayed almost during
the whole night to the Saint to restore my father's health.

After he took the oil, his water began to pass
like a stream. Simultaneously, the stones began to
come out one after the other. The next day, the
blood and the urine were tested. They were nor-
mal; and my father returned home full of health,
thanks to the miraculous power of the Saint.[7]

6

Mrs. Demetra A. Petrakou of Ambelochorion,
Laconia, relates the following:

In July, 1963, I was admitted to the Zanneion

Hospital at Piraeus, and was operated on the left breast, where I had a tumor. After my departure from the hospital, I took radiation treatments at the Anticancer Hospital "St. Savvas." But after 45 days a tumor appeared on my right breast, and you can imagine. . . .

At the Anticancer Hospital a lady urged me to pray to St. Nectarios, otherwise I would accomplish nothing. In my despair, I went to Aegina together with my husband, and prayed and entreated the Saint with my whole soul. We took oil from the sacred lamp of the Saint and crossed the tumor, and the tumor automatically disappeared. Glory to God![8]

7

Mr. Anastasios Raphtis, who lives at 17 Tsigante St. in Rhodes, writes that he began to suffer from his stomach ten years ago, and that from 1969 to February 1970 he experienced excruciating pains. He had X-rays taken, and his physicians told him that it was necessary for him to be operated on immediately for ulcer and gastritis.

But he was afraid, because he had a wife and children. In his despair, he prayed to Saint Nectarios, asking to be made well and promising to publish an account of his recovery in the periodical *Hagia Marina.*

After a few days, he went and prayed at the Church of Saint Nectarios in Archipolis, Rhodes, and gave his gold cross to be placed on the icon of the Saint as a votive offering. Since then the pains have ceased completely, and he is perfectly well. He thanks God and the Saint.[9]

WORKS OF THE SAINT

Published works are arranged under various headings in chronological order. Books are listed first, then pamphlets, and next articles. Unpublished works are listed after the published ones, in alphabetical order.

PUBLISHED WORKS

BOOKS AUTHORED

(1) *Deka Ekklesiastikoi Logoi dia ten Megalen Tessarakosten* ("Ten Sermons on the Great Lent"). Alexandria, 1885.

(2) *Peri ton Hieron Synodon kai idios peri tes Spoudaiotetos ton Dyo Proton Oikoumenikon Synodon* ("Concerning the Holy Synods and Es-

pecially Concerning the First Two Oecumenical Synods"). Alexandria, 1888.

(3) *Peri tes en to Kosmo Apokalypseos tou Theou* ("Concerning God's Revelation in the World"). Athens, 1892.

(4) *Ta Hiera Mnemosyna* ("Holy Memorial Services"). Athens, 1892.

(5) *Hai Oikoumenikai Synodoi tes tou Christou Ekklesias* ("The Oecumenical Synods of the Church of Christ"). Athens, 1892; Thessaloniki, 1972. This is a revised and enlarged edition of the book *Concerning the Holy Synods* listed above.

(6) *Hypotyposis peri Anthropou* ("Sketch Concerning Man"). Athens, 1893 and *ca.* 1975 (year not listed).

(7) *Peri Epimeleias Psyches* ("Concerning Care of the Soul"). Athens, 1894, 1973.

(8) *Peri ton Apotelesmaton tes Alethous kai Pseudous Morphoseos* ("Concerning the Results of True and Pseudo Education"). Athens, 1894.

(9) *Hieron kai Philosophikon Logion Thesaurisma* ("Treasury of Sacred and Philosophical Sayings"). 2 vols., Athens, 1895-1896.

(10) *Epikai kai Elegeiakai Gnomai ton Mikron Hellenon Poieton* ("Epic and Elegiac Maxims of the Minor Greek Poets"). Athens, 1896.

(11) *Encheiridon Christianikes Ethikes* ("Handbook of Christian Ethics"). Athens, 1897. 2nd edition, greatly augmented, entitled *Christianike Ethike tes Orthodoxou Anatolikes Ekklesias* ("Christian Ethics of the Eastern Orthodox Church"). Athens, 1965.

(12) *Mathema Poimantikes* ("Course in Pastoral Theology"). Athens, 1898, 1972.

(13) *Hiera Katechesis tes Anatolikes Orthodoxou Ekklesias* ("Sacred Catechism of the Eastern Orthodox Church"). Athens, 1899; Thessaloniki, 1972.

(14) *Christologia* ("Christology"). Athens, 1901 and *ca.* 1970.

(15) *Melete peri tes Athanasias tes Psyches kai peri ton Hieron Mnemosynon* ("Study Concerning the Immortality of the Soul and Concerning Holy Memorial Services"). Athens, 1901, 1972.

(16) *Euangelike Historia, di' Harmonias ton Keimenon ton Hieron Euangeliston Matthaiou, Markou, Louka kai Ioannou* ("The Gospel Story

through the Harmony of the Texts of the Holy
Evangelists Matthew, Mark, Luke and John").
Athens, 1903.

(17) *Proseuchetarion Katanyktikon* ("Book of
Contrite Prayers"). Athens, 1904. 2nd, enlarged
edition, Athens, 1913.

(18) *To Gnothi Sauton, etoi Meletai Threskeutikai kai Ethikai* ("Know Thyself, or Religious
and Ethical Studies"). Athens, 1904. 2nd edition,
Athens, 1962.

(19) *Melete peri Metanoias kai Exomologeseos*
("Study Concerning Repentance and Confession"). Athens, 1904.

(20) *Melete peri tes Metros tou Kyriou, tes
Hyperagias Theotokou kai Aeiparthenou Marias*
("Study Concerning the Mother of the Lord, the
Most Holy Theotokos and Evervirgin Mary").
Athens, 1904 and *ca.* 1970.

(21) *Melete peri tou Mysteriou tes Theias Eucharistias* ("Study Concerning the Mysterion of
the Divine Eucharist"). Athens, 1904.

(22) *Melete peri ton Hagion tou Theou*
("Study Concerning the Saints of God"). Athens,
1904 and *ca.* 1970.

(23) *Theotokarion, etoi Proseuchetarion Mikron* ("Book of Hymns to the Theotokos, or Small Book of Prayers"). Athens, 1905. 2nd, considerably enlarged, edition, entitled *Theotokarion*, Athens, 1907. Reprinted, Kastelli-Kissamou (Crete), 1967; Athens, 1972.

(24) *Hieratikon Engolpion* ("Priest's Manual"). Athens, 1907.

(25) *Triadikon, etoi Odai kai Hymnoi pros ton en Triadi Theon* ("Triadikon, or Odes and Hymns to the Triune God"). Athens, 1909.

(26) *Melete Historike peri ton Aition tou Schismatos, peri tes Diaioniseos Autou, kai peri tou Dynatou e Adynatou tes Henoseos ton Dyo Ekklesion, tes Anatolikes kai tes Dytikes* ("An Historical Study Concerning the Causes of the Schism, Concerning its Perpetuation, and Concerning the Possibility or Impossibility of the Union of the Two Churches, the Eastern and the Western"). 2 vols., Athens, 1911-1912.

(27) *Meletai Dyo: "A' Peri tes Mias Hagias Katholikes kai Apostolikes Ekklesias; B' Peri tes Hieras Paradoseos* ("Two Studies: I Concerning the One, Holy, Catholic and Apostolic Church; II Concerning Holy Tradition"). Athens, 1913 and *ca.* 1970.

(28) *Historike Melete peri tou Timiou Stau-rou* ("Historical Study Concerning the Precious Cross"). Athens, 1914 and *ca.* 1970.

(29) *Melete peri ton Theion Mysterion* ("Study Concerning the Divine Mysteria"). Athens, 1915 and *ca.* 1970.

BOOKS EDITED

(1) *Schediasma peri Anexithreskeias* ("Sketch Concerning Religious Tolerance") by Eugenios Voulgaris, 2nd edition. Alexandria, 1890.

(2) *Christianike Ethike* ("Christian Ethics") by Neophytos Vamvas. Alexandria, 1893.

(3) *Physike Theologia* ("Natural Theology") by Neophytos Vamvas. Alexandria, 1893.

(4) *Pandektes ton Theopneuston Hagion Gra-phon* ("Pandect of the Divinely Inspired Scriptures") by Antiochos, Monk of the Lavra of St. Savvas. Athens, 1908.

BOOKS PUT INTO VERSE

(1) *Psalterion tou Prophetanaktos Dauid, En-tetamenon eis Metra kata ten Toniken Basin, meta Hermeneutikon Semeioseon* ("The Psalter of the Prophet-King David Put into Verse in ac-

cordance with the Tonal Base, with Interpretative Notes"). Athens, 1906.

(2) *Kekragarion tou Theiou kai Hierou Augoustinou, Episkopou Hipponos, Entathen eis Metra kata ten Toniken Basin, ek tes Metaphraseos tou Eugeniou tou Boulgareos* ("The Book *Unto Thee I have Cried* of the Divine and Holy Augustine, Bishop of Hippo, Put into Verse in accordance with the Tonal Base, following the Translation of Eugenios Voulgaris"). 2 vols., Athens, 1910.

PAMPHLETS

(1) *Logos Ekklesiastikos, A' Kyriake ton Nesteion, Peri Pisteos* ("Sermon, on the First Sunday of the Fasts, Concerning Faith"). Athens, 1885.

(2) *Logos Ekklesiastikos, D' Kyriake ton Nesteion, Peri Exomologeseos* ("Sermon, on the Fourth Sunday of the Fasts, Concerning Confession"). Athens, 1885.

(3) *Logos Ekklesiastikos, E' Kyriake ton Nesteion, Peri Theias Eucharistias* ("Sermon, on the Fifth Sunday of the Fasts, Concerning the Divine Eucharist"). Athens, 1885.

(4) *Logos Ekklesiastikos eis ten Megalen Para-skeuen* ("Sermon on Great Friday"). Athens, 1885.

(5) *Logos Ekklesiastikos te Kyriake tes Apokreo peri Metanoias* ("Sermon on the Sunday of Apo-kreo Concerning Repentance"). Athens, 1885.

(6) *Melete epi tes Psyches tou Anthropou kai tou Zoou* ("Study on the Soul of Man and of the Animal"). Athens, 1885.

(7) *Peri tes Alethous Eleutherias kai tes Sche-seos Autes pros ten Ethiken Eleutherian* ("Concerning True Freedom and its Relation to Moral Freedom"). Athens, 1885.

(8) *Peri tes en Pneumati kai Aletheia Latreias* ("Concerning Worship in Spirit and in Truth"). Athens, 1885.

(9) *Peri tes pros ton Theon Agapes kai Latreias* ("Concerning the Love and Worship of God"). Athens, 1885.

(10) *Peri Hypomones en tais Thlipsesin* ("Concerning Patient Endurance in Afflictions"). Athens, 1885.

(11) *Dyo Logoi Ekklesiastikoi: Logos A', Eis ten Kyriaken tes Orthodoxias, etoi Peri Pisteos; Logos B', Peri tes en to Kosmo Apokalypseos tou Theou,*

etoi Peri Thaumaton ("Two Sermons: Sermon I, On the Sunday of Orthodoxy, or Concerning Faith; Sermon II, Concerning God's Revelation in the World, or Concerning Miracles"). Cairo, 1887.

(12) *Logos Ekphonetheis en to Achillopouleio Parthenagogeio kata ten Heorten ton Trion Hierarchon* ("Address Delivered at the Achillopoulion School for Girls on the Feast of the Three Hierarchs"). Alexandria, 1889.

ARTICLES

(1) *Melete peri ton Hagion Eikonon* ("Study Concerning the Holy Icons"), in the periodical *Anamorphosis*, 1902, Vol. 4, No. 26, pp. 202-204, No. 27, pp. 210-212, No. 28, pp. 218-221, No. 29, pp. 226-228, No. 30, pp. 234-236, No. 31 pp. 244-246, No. 32, pp. 250-251, No. 33, pp. 258-260, No. 34, pp. 266-268, No. 35, p. 274, No. 36, pp. 282-283.

(2) *Peri Horkou* ("Concerning Oath"), in the periodical *Hieros Syndesmos*, 1906, Vol. 10, No. 25, pp. 7-8, No. 26, pp. 7-9, No. 27, pp. 8-9. Reprinted in pamphlet form by Archimandrite Titos Matthaiakis in 1955.

(3) *Melete peri Ekklesias* ("Study Concerning the Church"), in the Festive Volume celebrating the 75th anniversary (1844-1919) of the Rizarios School, Athens, 1920, pp. 334-349.

(4) *He Theia Leitourgia tou Hagiou kai Endoxou Apostolou kai Euangelistou Markou* ("The Divine Liturgy of the Holy and Glorious Apostle and Evangelist Mark"), in the periodical *Theologia,* 1955, Vol. 26, No. 1, pp. 14-36. Edited by Matthaiakis.

(5) *Historike Melete peri ton Diatetagmenon Nesteion* ("An Historical Study Concerning the Ordained Fasts"), in *Theologia,* 1956, Vol. 27, No. 3, pp. 463-480. Edited by Matthaiakis.

(Many other writings of St. Nectarios appeared during his lifetime in religious periodicals such as *Anamorphosis, Anaplasis,* and *Hieros Syndesmos.* Among these were some of his books that have been listed above.)

LETTERS

Over sixty letters of the Saint have been published by Archimandrite Titos Matthaiakis in his book *Saint Nectarios Kephalas.* Of greatest interest perhaps are the following seven, of which the first six were written for the nuns of his Convent in Aegina before he withdrew there, while the last is addressed to the monk Ioasaph:

(1) *Peri Agathes Syneideseos* ("On Good Conscience"), Matthaiakis, *op. cit.*, pp. 195-199.

(2) *Peri Allages ton Onomaton ton Monachon* ("On the Change of the Names of Monastics"), pp. 217-219.

(3) *Peri Katharas Kardias kai Pneumatos* ("On Purity of Heart and Spirit"), pp. 220-222.

(4) *Peri Eirenes Psyches* ("On Peace of Soul"), pp. 225-227.

(5) *Homilia peri Aretes* ("Homily on Virtue"), pp. 241-244.

(6) *Peri Agapes pros Christon* ("On Love for Christ"), pp. 244-246.

(7) *Epistole pros Monachon* ("Letter to a Monk"), pp. 260-262.

Unpublished Works

(1) *Chrestomatheia* (Book of moral selections).

(2) *Enkyklopaideia tes Philosophias* ("Encyclopedia of Philosophy").

(3) *Heortologia tes Orthodoxou Anatolikes*

Ekklesias ("Calendar of Holy Days of the Eastern Orthodox Church"), divided into two parts, of which the first pertains to the Sundays of the entire year, while the second pertains to the fixed and the movable holy days.

(4) *Hermeneia ton Praxeon ton Apostolon* ("Interpretation of the Acts of the Apostles").

(5) *Hiera Leitourgike* ("Sacred Liturgics").

(6) *Historias Ekklesiastikes Mystike Theoria* ("Mystical View of Church History").

(7) *Kephalaia Pente peri ton Leitourgikon Biblion* ("Five Chapters on the Liturgical Books").

(8) *Melete peri ton Hagion Leipsanon* ("Study on Sacred Relics").

(9) *Neon Paschalion Aionion* (New table listing the month and the day when Pascha is celebrated each year throughout the century).

(10) *Neon Triadikon* (New book of hymns to the Holy Trinity).

(11) *Peri Hellenismou* ("Concerning Hellenism").

(12) *Peri Kerou Melisses kai Elaiou hos Prosphoras, kai peri Thymiamatos* ("Concerning Bees-

wax and Oil as Offerings, and Concerning Incense").

(13) *Peri Mesaionos kai tou Byzantinou Hellenismou* ("Concerning the Medieval Period and Byzantine Hellenism").

(14) *Peri tes Aphieroseos to Theo Hosion Parthenon, kai peri Monon kai Monachikou Biou* ("Concerning the Dedication of Holy Virgins to God, and Concerning Monasteries and the Monastic Life").

ON GOD

A God-centered author, a personality anchored in God, St. Nectarios refers often to God in all his writings. He has devoted three of his books to the topic of God. They are: *Concerning God's Revelation in the World*, which was published in 1892, when he was a preacher in Euboia; *Christology*, which was published in 1901, when he was Director of the Rizarios Ecclesiastical School; and *Triadikon, or Odes and Hymns to the Holy Trinity*, which appeared in 1909, when he was leading a monastic life in Aegina. Also, he devoted to the subject of God a significant part of three other works: *The Oecumenical Synods of the Church of Christ, Treasury of Sacred and Philosophical Sayings,* and *Sacred Catechism of the Eastern Orthodox Church*. The first appeared in 1892; the second, during the years 1895 and 1896; the third in 1899.

Indicative of the primacy which the blessed
Nectarios gives to the topic of God is the fact that
the first volume of his *Treasury of Sacred and
Philosophical Sayings* begins with chapters that
consist of collections of passages concerning faith
in God, while the first forty pages of the second
volume, after the Preface, are an anthology of passages that pertain to God. In this manner, St. Nectarios emphasizes that we must begin with God.
In order to be more emphatic in this, he quotes
on the first page sayings under the heading: "That
we must begin with God." This is reminiscent of
a similar exhortation of St. Cosmas Aitolos: "It is
proper and reasonable, my fellow Christians, as
we learn from the Holy Book of the Gospels and
the other Scriptures, that we begin our teaching
with God." In his *Sacred Catechism* St. Nectarios
similarly begins, immediately after the Introduction, with the topic of God.

In all the books that have been mentioned, philosophical reflection, dialectic, accompanies the
exposition of revealed truth. A deeply philosophical mind, and versed in secular philosophy, he
selected from philosophy, chiefly that of ancient
Greece, whatever was useful for his work as a theologian — like the bee, according to the counsel

of Basil the Great and John Damascene. The bee, observe these two Fathers, takes from flowers what is useful to it for producing honey, and disregards whatever is useless. Thus, secular philosophy is put to the service of theology, becomes her handmaid.

Let us see what he says in the above mentioned six works, following the order in which they have been cited.

In the first book that is devoted in its entirety to God, *Concerning God's Revelation in the World,* the Saint sets as his aim to prove that God reveals Himself to mankind. He holds that God's revelation to man is achieved in two ways: (a) *indirectly* and (b) *directly. Indirect* revelation is effected through creatures, is apprehended by means of the sense-organs, that is, sight hearing, and so on. It is of two kinds: (i) through *miracles,* and (ii) through *creation.*

He undertakes to prove dialectically that: "Miracles are not impossible from a logical standpoint, and that right reason does not deny them; . . . and that miracles are a consequence of the Creator's love for his own creature, whom God does not abandon but leads to a designed meaningful end."[1]

The Saint repeatedly stresses that God's revelation, both through miracles and other means, is a consequence of His love, of His goodness. Extoling God's love for man, he says: "God as Creator loves His own creature, but He has especially love for man, whom He created in His image and likeness, in order to render him a partaker of His own goodness and blessedness."[2]

Through miracles, God "as it were prompts man to a knowledge of His will, and a return to Him, because in Him is found perfection, for which he has been destined."[3]

With regard to the second type of indirect revelation, that through *creation,* the holy Father makes the following beautiful and wise observation: "From the least to the greatest of creatures, all declare the wisdom, the power, the goodness, and the justice of the Creator."[4] This passage brings to my mind a similar observation which was made by a saintly hermit whom I met some twenty years ago at Karoulia of Mount Athos. His name was Philaretos. In the course of a conversation that I had with him, I noted that he saw every-

where around him the almightiness and goodness
of God: in the awe-inspiring rock of the wilder-
ness where he dwelt, in the scattered shrubs that
were wedged in it, the few wild flowers, his tiny
vegetable garden, and the deep blue sea below.
"Look," he said, pointing at a potato plant in his
garden. "You take a potato and bury it in the soil
and out of it grows a plant with beautiful leaves
and flowers, and a cluster of other potatoes. How
marvellous! And if the all-good God produces
such wonderful things here, how much greater
marvels await those who shall enter Heaven. O!
How good God is, and how grateful we ought to
feel towards Him!"[5]

About revelation through creation, St. Nectarios observes that it may be viewed as "the usual
way through which God reveals Himself daily to
man."[6]

Direct revelation is, like indirect revelation, of
two kinds, according to our Saint: (i) that which
is through *inspiration,* and (ii) that which is
through *association.* Through inspiration (*em-
pneusis*), "God manifests Himself to His elect one
and converses with him, as one does with his personal friend.[7] This revelation becomes known to
us through consciousness.

The revelation of God through *inspiration* is more perfect than revelation through miracles and that through creation. Through it, God illuminates the perfect. It is through inspiration that the Prophets spoke of the coming of the Savior Jesus Christ and of other important events. "Moved by the Divine Spirit," says St. Nectarios, "the holy men of God spoke and said that it was the Holy Spirit Who talked through their mouth."[8] That they really spoke inspired by the Holy Spirit is verified by the fact that all their prophecies "were completely fulfilled."[9]

The second form of direct revelation of God, that through *association* (*prosoikeiosis*) is, according to St. Nectarios, the most perfect. "Through it," he says, "man perceives spiritually God and is conscious of the indwelling of God, according to the saying of the Lord, "I shall dwell in you, and walk, and make my abode with you."[10] Association is effected "through the human mind's approach to, and communion with, the Divine Logos. This communion takes place through consciousness, in which cognition, feeling, and the will united together reach their highest point. Through this culmination man rises above the realm where he has only an abstract idea of God and attains to

another realm, where particular things are no
longer present, but he meets directly God, the
Divine Logos Himself, in Whom there are all the
Divine ideas and the power of realizing them and
bringing creatures into existence. There he finally
comes into direct real communion with Him and
hears His voice."[11]

Like the other types of revelation, this also has
as its aim the perfection of man. Our Saint remarks in this connection: "God has bestowed this
approach upon mankind, in order that it might be
deified through spiritualization."[12]

The possibility of such a revelation, where man
is united with God is confirmed, according to the
holy Father, by the spiritual nature of man,
through which "man occupies an altogether exceptional place, and may be called the king among
creatures and the crown of creation."[13]

With regard to the manner through which association is achieved, St. Nectarios teaches that
there is required true knowledge of God and of
the Divine will, that is, Orthodoxy, the fulfillment
of the Divine will with all our powers, aided in
this by Divine grace. "He who rightly knows the
Deity and His will," says the Saint, "and with all

his strength seeks to fulfill it, succeeds with Divine help in freeing himself of all that is base and low-minded, in rising to a higher realm and associating with the Deity."[14]

What St. Nectarios calls here the "association" or "communion" of man with God is called by the Church Fathers *theosis*, "deification" or "divinization." He speaks of it as *apotheosis*, and teaches that it is attained through our purification and the perfect identification of our will with the Divine will.[15]

Our Saint returns to the subject in later works. He speaks there more analytically of theosis and of the conditions under which it is attained, employing words and phrases which we encounter in the writings of the "Wakeful Fathers" (*Neptikoi Pateres*), such as John Climacos, Symeon the New Theologian, and Gregory Palamas. For example, he speaks of "effulgence" (*ellampsis*), "illumination" (*photismos*), and "the Divine light" (*to theion phos*). Thus, in his book *Know Thyself*, which was first published in 1905, he says: "God reveals Himself to the humble who practice virtue."[16] God does not reveal Himself, he remarks, through the imagination, which has no place in that experience. "No imagination can represent the supernal and ultramundane," he says. "Imagination produces only illusions. It neither leads to Heaven, nor presents the illusionist to God, nor reveals mysteries, but deludes the foolish, representing fictitious images; and it corrupts their foolish souls."[17] The "supernal and ultramundane," that is, the Divine, becomes perceptible only "through the effulgence of Divine grace."[18] In a letter that was published in Archimandrite Titos Matthaiakis' *Saint Nectarios Kephalas* (1955), St. Nectarios says: "The Divine light illumines the pure heart and the pure intellect, because these are receptive of light; but impure hearts and intellects, not being receptive of illumination, abhor the light of knowledge, the light of truth. . . . A guileless and pure heart is something great, because it is receptive of the Divine light and of Divine revelations."[19]

The second book of the Saint that is devoted to the topic of God, *Christology,* has as its aim the defense of the divinity of Christ, and through this defense the strengthening of faith in Him. To achieve this, he develops systematically the Orthodox teaching concerning the incarnate Divine Logos, concerning the testimonies which confirm the truth of Christianity, such as the miracles performed by Christ and the fulfillment of the prophecies regarding His coming.

Christology is a work written with great love and reverence for our Lord, and in an engaging style. It begins with the topic: "Concerning the Son of man; that Jesus Christ is the way, the truth, and the life." Quoting the statement: "I am the way, the truth, and the life" (John 14: 6), the Saint observes: "What gladsome words! What authority in them! How wonderful and good to hear are these words! What longed for good news for men! The words are full of life, full of satisfaction for the longings of the hearts of men. . . . 'I am the way, the truth, and the life!' They contain a whole treasure, a treasure that enriches the whole of mankind. In them is contained the totality of the longings of mankind from the earliest times."[20]

Continuing, he says: "Men were seeking a way, truth, and life; this fervid longing of mankind God fulfilled by sending His only-begotten Son. . . . Mankind longed for the coming of the promised Savior, Teacher, and Redeemer. The prophets had announced beforehand, divinely inspired men foretold, His coming. . . . The words of the Savior: 'I am the way, the truth, and the life,' are a proc-

lamation of His coming; they are a reply to mankind that was waiting for Him; they are a testimony of the issue and fulfillment of the predic-
tions and the prophecies. . . . They were a relief
for weary souls and light for those in darkness;
they were hope for those in despair and joy for the
afflicted. . . ."[21]

In the chapters of Part One that follow, the holy
Father speaks about the necessity of faith in Christ
and about its power, about His work of redemption, about the divinity of Christ, about His two
natures, the divine and the human — that "being
perfect God, He became perfect man" — and
about the fact that God Who reveals Himself in
the Old Testament under the name of Jehovah is
the Son of God the Father, the Logos of God, the
second person of the Holy Trinity, that is, Jesus
Christ, not the Father."

From the beginning to the end, *Christology* is
fully documented with references to Holy Scripture and the writings of the Fathers and other
Church writers. Thus it is evident that St. Nectarios does not present subjective, simply personal
opinions, but the authentic teaching of the Orthodox Church.

Also manifest in that book is the Christocentric character of the Saint's thought. This is discernible in his other writings, too. A consequence of this is the emphasis which he places on the unceasing invocation of the name of Christ. In an article that has the form of a letter addressed to Eusebia the Nun, he says: "The virgin who has come to love Christ and is dedicated to Him and lives for Him, no longer lives for herself, but Christ lives in her. . . . She converses with Him and gazes at Him, lifts up her heart and intellect towards Him. Her pure lips utter His sweetest name at all times, and from her bosom are sent up warm sighs, as unceasing hymns sent up to the heights of Divine love. His Divine name has become the unceasing meditation of her heart that has been wounded by Divine love. Every pulsation of her heart sends up a prayer. Her breath is ever accompanied by an invocation of the Divine name."[22] Although he is addressing himself to a nun, there is no doubt that he would have made the same statements to every Christian who aspired to attain perfection, theosis, salvation. The form of prayer which he recommends is known in the Orthodox hesychast tradition as the "Jesus Prayer," and is usually limited to the words: "Lord Jesus Christ, Son of God, have mercy upon me." It is also called "mental (*noera*)

prayer" and "prayer of the heart," because it is
performed mentally, by the rational faculty, in the
heart, the emotional center of man. This prayer
is especially recommended by the great Wakeful
Fathers, such as, in modern times, St. Nicodemos
the Hagiorite. Nicodemos says, characteristically:
"Let Jesus, I entreat you, be the sweet meditation
of your heart." A great number of relevant texts
have been gathered together in the famous *Philokalia*. There are indications in the writings of St.
Nectarios that he had studied the *Philokalia* and
enriched his knowledge and spiritual life through
the study of this important work.[23]

Besides the two books in which he deals with
the subject of God in a scholarly manner, the blessed Father also wrote, as we have noted, a book
of hymns and odes to the Holy Trinity, the *Triadikon*. He explains in the Preface, that they
"were prompted by the feeling of worship, and
by the longing to praise God in hymns;" and their
publication, by the desire to satisfy "the religious
feeling of pious Greek Orthodox Christians who
wish to worship the Holy Trinity with hymns and
odes."

These poems, which evoke admiration for the
poetic talent of the Saint, present sublime truths,

doctrinal teachings about God and His relation to man, and at the same time feelings of repentance and compunction before the all-good, all-wise, and omnipotent God. They are embellished with elegant expressions. As representative examples of this poetic creation, I shall give a few verses from his "Hymn of Entreaty" and one of the Odes (pp. 34-35). He says in the first:

> "Offer a sacrifice of praise to God,
> O soul, that of doing what is good,
> while there is still time."

> "There approaches, O soul,
> the cutting off by death.
> Hasten to do worthy deeds,
> lest thou be cut off like the fig-tree."

In the Ode he says:

> "Thou Who dost will mercy, have mercy upon
> those who with faith take refuge in Thee.
> Grant forgiveness of their offences,
> and deliver them from passions and dangers.

> "In the ineffable sea of Thy goodness,
> bestow upon me the light-giving splendor
> of Thy divine effulgence, O eternal
> light-giving Spiritual Sun.

"Let us glorify the consubstantial Trinity:
the beginningless Father, the co-eternal Son,
the All-Holy Spirit — one kingdom,
one essence and one lordship."

Now let us see what the Saint teaches in the re-
maining three works which I mentioned, in which
he does not deal exclusively with the subject of
God. In his book *The Oecumenical Synods of the
Church of Christ,* he explains the institution of
the Holy and Great Synods, the need for convok-
ing them, the history of each of the Seven Oecumenical Synods, and their valuable contribution
to the Orthodox Church. In the description of
each Synod, he explains the reasons that led to the
convocation of it, namely, the particular heresies,
as well as the manner in which they opposed, ra-
tionally and courageously, the false doctrines of
the heretics, and how, through definitions and
canons, "the true faith was safeguadred, the authentic spirit of Christ's Church Militant was preserved incorrupt, truth itself was demonstrated,
and Orthodoxy triumphed."[24] The Seven Oecumenical Synods were convoked for the purpose of
confronting problems of dogma, of safeguarding
the Church from heretical teachings. Except for
the Seventh Oecumenical Synod, which was held

for confronting the Iconoclasts, the rest of the
Oecumenical Synods, as St. Nectarios shows very
clearly, were convoked for opposing heresies with
regard to the subject of God. He explains in de-
tail the various heresies, and gives the formulation
of the Orthodox doctrine in the case of each Synod.
He unreservedly espouses the decisions of the Synods. Thus the divine Nectarios shows himself in
this, as well as in his other works about which I
have spoken, a profound and authentic Orthodox
theologian.

He sums up the contribution of each Oecumenical Synod as follows:

The First, "convoked against Arius, *confessed
the son of man to be the Son of God,* and declared
Him *to be of one essence with the Father and co-
eternal.*"[25]

The Second, "convoked against Macedonius
who fought against the Holy Spirit, . . . declared,
on the one hand *the unity of the Triadic God,* and
on the other hand *the Divinity of the Son and of
the Holy Spirit, the third person of the Holy Trinity,* which (Trinity) was revealed to us through
Christ."[26]

The Third Oecumenical Synod "opposed the misunderstanding of the preceding two Synods by Nestorius and others, validating their dogmas, . . . and defined the connection and manner of *union of the two natures of Christ, the Divine and the human, and confessed the All-Holy Virgin Mary as Theotokos* (Godbirthgiver) ."[27]

The Fourth Oecumenical Synod, "having assembled against *Eutyches and Dioskouros of Alexandria, opposed the dogma of Monophysitism,* whereby the human nature of Christ was absorbed by the Divine, and there was recognized only one of his natures, the Divine; and it *confessed that our Lord Jesus Christ is perfect God and perfect man.*"[28]

The Fifth, "which took place *against Origen and the Three Chapters,*" ratified the one right faith, which had been confessed by the preceding four holy Synods, and repulsed the accusation that they inclined towards Nestorianism."[29]

Finally, the Sixth, which was held against the Monothelites, proved that in Jesus Christ, Who has two natures, the Divine and the human, there are two wills, "namely, the Divine will and the human will, and that the human will submits to the Divine."[30]

Thus, in the work *The Oecumenical Synods of the Church of Christ,* there is an exact exposition of the Orthodox teaching concerning the Holy Trinity and a condemnation of the related ancient heresies.

It is well to add here that the blessed Father, upholding fully all that was formulated and proclaimed regarding God by the Oecumenical Synods, took a clear stand on the heresy of the *filioque* — the dogma that the Holy Spirit proceeds not only from the Father, but also from the Son — which in 1014 was decreed by the Western Church. In Vol. 2 of his work *Historical Study Concerning the Causes of the Schism,* which was published in 1912, St. Nectarios criticizes this addition to the Symbol of the Faith. "An addition to the holy Symbol," he stresses, "is not permissible, because the dogma concerning the faith in the Holy Trinity was formulated perfectly by th holy Fathers"[31] of the Oecumenical Synods. He adds that the Orthodox Church acknowledges "the divine character and holiness of their dogmas."[32]

Reference has already been made to the work
Treasury of Sacred and Philosophical Sayings.
Here, our Saint gathered together a vast number
of sayings on numerous topics, taking them from
Holy Scripture, from the Fathers of the Church,
from philosophers, poets and other writers, ancient and modern, chiefly Greek. Many sections
of this two-volume work pertain to God. In them
is taught that we must begin with God, that God
exists, that He is almighty, unchanging, omnisci-
ent, just, merciful, long-suffering, and so on.
Also, there is taught the need of man's turning to
God and entering into relation with Him through
faith, hope, love, and piety.

Finally, let us see what St. Nectarios teaches
about God in his *Sacred Catechism of the Eastern
Orthodox Church*. In the first place, summing up
the teaching of the Church concerning the existence of God, he says that "there exists one God,
creator of heaven and earth, and of all things
therein, that is, the creator of intelligible and sensible nature." Regarding this we have, he says, as
our sources, "those of natural and of supernatural
revelation." Natural revelation is "the revelation
of His wisdom, power, goodness, and glory in
the works of creation."[33] Supernatural revelation

is "the direct revelation of God to man in a supernatural manner."[34]

Holy Scripture, that is, the Old and the New
Testament, speaks of these two kinds of revelation. Regarding natural revelation, Psalm 18 (Septuagint), for example, says: "The heavens declare
the glory of God; and the firmament showeth His
handiwork." And the Epistle to the Romans says:
"The invisible things of Him from the creation
of the world are clearly seen, being understood by
the things that are made, even His eternal power
and Godhead."[35] As far as supernatural revelation
is concerned, our Saint observes that "all the pages
of Holy Scripture are full of testimonies of God's
supernatural revelation."[36] The highest testimony
of it is "the incarnation of the Logos of God and
the descent of the Holy Spirit."[37]

From natural revelation, continues the holy
Father, we receive the following arguments for
the existence of God: (a) the Anthropological,
(b) the Ontological, (c) the Cosmological, (d)
the Teleological, (e) the Moral, and (f) the Historical.[38] And from supernatural revelation we
receive the Religious argument, which is the
logical conclusion drawn from the mystical rev-

elation of God in the believer. This is analyzable into these proofs: (a) from feeling, (b) from love, (c) from Divine grace and power, (d) from the fruits of the Holy Spirit, (e) from the gifts of the Holy Spirit, and (f) from the illumination of the intellect.[39]

Next, he distinguishes between the "essence" of God and His "attributes." The essence (*ousia*) of God is incomprehensible and inexpressible. His attributes (*idiomata*), that is, "His distinguishing characteristics," become known to man through the twofold revelation, the natural and the supernatural. Scripture mentions, among others, the following attributes of God, observes the divine Hierarch: bliss, wisdom, omniscience, foreknowledge, omnipotence, goodness, love, justice, and holiness.

From the general conception of God that has been set forth above, St. Nectarios proceeds to the concrete Orthodox teaching about the Holy Trinity, drawing from the Bible and the Symbol of the Faith. In the Symbol, which he explains in a detailed manner, "there were formulated," he says, "the truths which the Church received from the Holy Apostles, the Disciples of our Savior Christ."[40]

According to the Orthodox teaching, "in the essence of the one God there are distinguishable three Hypostases, or three Persons: the Father, the Son, and the Holy Spirit."[41] These three Persons are related as follows: "The Father is the cause of the Son and of the Spirit. . . . The Father begets the Son non-temporally, that is, before all ages, and He sends forth (*proballe*) the Holy Spirit; the Son is born of the Father, and the Holy Spirit proceeds eternally from the Father. In addition, the Church teaches and professes one principle in the Deity, and acknowledges one cause of the Son and of the Spirit: the Father. It holds that the infinite essence of the Father is also the essence of the Son and of the Holy Spirit; and that the Father, the Son and the Holy Spirit are one God, and one indivisible essence and nature."[42]

The three Persons, continues the Saint, "as being of the same essence and nature, have all the same Divine attributes, mind that is all-wise, will that is almighty, and the feeling of absolute and perfect love. They are distinguished from one another only through their personal attributes. These are, in the case of the Father, that He is not begotten of anyone and does not proceed from anyone, but is Himself the principle and cause, the source and root of the other two Hypostases;" in the case of the Son, that He is begotten of the Father; and of the Holy Spirit, that He proceeds from the Father.[43]

"Considered in relation to creatures, particularly man and his salvation, the Holy Trinity is called dispensational (oikonomike). Its relation towards creatures and especially man is one of love, even towards men who are sinners and unworthy of love. From this dispensational standpoint, the second Person of the Holy Trinity, the Son, is called the Logos of the Father or simply the Logos, because He is the mouth of the Father for men, His full and speedy revelation, through Whom God the Father revealed Himself, His volitions and mysteries to men."[44] From the same standpoint, the third Person is called the Holy Spirit (Pneuma), "as being a spiritual wind (pneuma) that fills the hearts of the faithful with life and spiritual grace. He is called Holy, in contrast to the evil and impure spirits, which also act in the world, seeking to defile man. The Holy Spirit is also called the Comforter (Parakletos) , as protecting and helping the faithful, so that they might fulfill their destiny of earth,"[45] attain salvation.

This, briefly, is the teaching of the most God-loving St. Nectarios of Aegina concerning God.

SELECTED PASSAGES FROM
THE WRITINGS OF THE SAINT

Christianity

Christian religion is not a certain philosophic system, about which learned men, trained in metaphysical studies, argue and then either espouse or reject, according to the opinion each one has formed. It is faith, established in the souls of men, which ought to be spread to the many and be maintained in their consciousnesses.[1]

* * *

There are truths in Christianity that are above our intellectual comprehension, incapable of being grasped by the finite mind of man. Our intellect takes cognizance of them, becomes convinced of their reality, and testifies about their supernatural existence.[2]

       *   *   *

Christianity is a religion of revelation. The Divine reveals its glory only to those who have been perfected through virtue. Christianity teaches perfection through virtue and demands that its followers become holy and perfect. It disapproves of and opposes those who are under the influence of the imagination. He who is truly perfect in virtue becomes through Divine help outside the flesh and the world, and truly enters another, spiritual world; not, however, through the imagination, but through the effulgence of Divine grace. Without grace, without revelation, no man, even the most virtuous, can transcend the flesh and the world.[3]

       *   *   *

God reveals Himself to the humble, who live in accordance with virtue. Those who take up the wings of the imagination attempt the flight of Ikaros and have the same end. Those who harbor phantasies do not pray; for he that prays lifts his mind and heart towards God, whereas he that turns to phantasies diverts himself. Those who are addicted to the imagination have withdrawn from God's grace and from the realm of Divine revelation. They have abandoned the heart in which grace is revealed and have surrendered themselves to the imagination, which is devoid of all grace. It is only the heart that receives knowledge about things that are not apprehended by the senses, because God, Who dwells and moves within it, speaks within it and reveals to it the substance of things hoped for.[4]

*   *   *

No imagination can represent the supernal and ultramundane, the things that belong to the spiritual world, because they are not objects of our senses. These things are revealed by God only to those who are pure in heart and mind.[5]

*   *   *

Seek God daily. But seek Him in your heart, not outside it. And when you find Him, stand with fear and trembling, like the Cherubim and the Seraphim, for your heart has become a throne of God. But in order to find God, become humble as dust before the Lord, for the Lord abhors the proud, whereas He visits those that are humble in heart, wherefore He says: "To whom will I look, but to him that is meek and humble in heart?"[6]

*   *   *

The Divine light illumines the pure heart and the pure intellect, because these are susceptible of receiving light; whereas impure hearts and intellects, not being susceptible of receiving illumination, have an aversion for the light of knowledge, the light of truth; they like darkness. . . . God loves those who have a pure heart, listens to their prayers, grants them their requests that lead to salvation, reveals Himself to them and teaches the mysteries of the Divine nature.[7]

The Church

The term Church, according to the strict Orthodox view, has two meanings, one of them expressing its doctrinal and religious character, that is, its inner, peculiarly spiritual essence, and the other expressing its external character. Thus, according to the Orthodox confession, the Church is defined in a twofold manner: as a religious institution, and as a religious community (*koinonia*).

The definition of the Church as a religious institution may be formulated thus: The Church is a divine religious institution of the New Testament, built by our Savior Jesus Christ through His incarnate Dispensation, established upon faith in Him and the true confession, and inaugurated on the day of holy Pentecost by the descent

of the All-Holy Spirit upon the holy Disciples and
Apostles of the Savior Christ, whom He rendered
instruments of Divine grace for the perpetuation
of his work of redemption. In this institution is
entrusted the totality of revealed truths; in it op-
erates Divine grace through the Mysteria; in it
are regenerated those who with faith approach
Christ the Savior; in it has been preserved both
the written and the unwritten Apostolic teaching
and tradition.

The definition of the Church as a religious
community may be formulated thus: The Church
is a society of men united in the unity of the
Spirit, in the bond of peace.[8]

*   *   *

In the broader Christian sense, the term Church
is the community of all the rational and free beings who believe in the Savior, including the angels, which (community), as the Apostle Paul
says, is "the body of Christ, the fulness of Him
that filleth all in all" (Eph. 1: 10 and 20-23), and
which includes also those who believed in Christ
prior to His coming and constituted the Church
of the Old Testament. This Church was guided,
during the time of the Patriarchs, by the prom-
ises and the faith based on revelation, and during

the time of Moses and the Prophets by the Law and the prophecies.[9]

* * *

The right view of the Church is that the Church is distinguished into the Militant and the Triumphant; and that it is Militant so long as it struggles against wickedness for the prevalence of the good, and Triumphant in the heavens, where there dwells the choir of the Righteous, who struggled and were made perfect in the faith in God and in virtue.[10]

Tradition

Sacred Tradition is the very Church; without the Sacred Tradition the Church does not exist. Those who deny the Sacred Tradition deny the Church and the preaching of the Apostles.

Before the writing of the Holy Scriptures, that is, of the sacred texts of the Gospels, the Acts and the Epistles of the Apostles, and before they were spread to the churches of the world, the Church was based on Sacred Tradition. . . . The holy texts are in relation to Sacred Tradition what the part is to the whole.[11]

* * *

The Church Fathers regard Sacred Tradition

as the safe guide in the interpretation of Holy
Scripture and absolutely necessary for understanding the truths contained in Holy Scripture.
The Church received many traditions from the
Apostles. . . . The constitution of the church services, especially of the Divine Liturgy, the holy
Mysteria themselves and the manner of perform-
ing them, certain prayers and other institutions of
the Church go back to that Sacred Tradition of
the Apostles.

In their conferences, the Holy Synods draw not
only from the Holy Scriptures, but also from
Sacred Tradition as from a pure fount. Thus, the
Seventh Oecumenical Synod says in its 8th De-
cree: "If one violates any part of the Church
Tradition, either written or unwritten, let him be
anathema."[12]

Discovering God

The pure heart perceives God and discovers
Him where the guileful heart cannot see Him
even when He is shown.[13]

*   *   *

It is evident that unbelief is an evil offspring
of an evil heart; for the guileless and pure heart

everywhere discovers God, everywhere discerns Him, and always unhesitatingly believes in His existence. When the man of pure heart looks at the World of Nature, that is, at the sky, the earth, and the sea and at all things in them, and observes the systems constituting them, the infinite multitude of stars of heaven, the innumerable multitudes of birds and quadrupeds and every kind of animal of the earth, the variety of plants on it, the abundance of fish in the sea, he is immediately amazed and exclaims with the Prophet David: "How great are Thy works, O Lord! in wisdom hast Thou made them all." Such a man, impelled by his pure heart, discovers God also in the World of Grace of the Church, from which the evil man is far removed. The man of pure heart believes in the Church, admires her spiritual system, discovers God in the Mysteria, in the heights of theology, in the light of Divine revelations, in the truths of the teachings, in the commandments of the Law, in the achievements of the Saints, in every good deed, in every perfect gift, and in general in the whole of creation. Justly then did the Lord say in His Beatitudes of those possessing purity of heart: "Blessed are the pure in heart, for they shall see God."[14]

Self-knowledge

Self-knowledge is man's foremost duty. Man, as a rational, morally free and religious being, is a being of lofty rank and has been destined to become like God, in Whose image he was created, and a participant in Divine goodness and blessedness. But in order to become a divine likeness, good and blessed, and to commune with God, man must first of all know himself. Without self-knowledge man goes astray in his thoughts, is dominated by diverse passions, tyrannized by violent desires, troubled about many and vain things, and leads a disorderly, distracted life, erring in all things, wandering on the way, staggering at every step; and he stumbles, falls, and is crushed. He drinks every day potions of sorrow and bitterness, fills his heart with grief, and lives an unbearable life.[16]

He who does not know himself does not know God, either. And he who does not know God does not know the truth and the nature of things in general. . . . He who does not know himself continually sins against God and continually moves farther away from Him. He who does not know the nature of things and what they truly are in themselves is powerless to evaluate them according to their worth and to discriminate between the mean and the precious, the worthless and the valuable. Wherefore, such a person wears himself out in the pursuit of vain and trivial things, and is unconcerned about and indifferent to the things that are eternal and most precious.

There is in man by nature the power of self-knowledge, because man is a spiritual and morally free being, having free will and the power of knowing. . . . But in order to acquire perfect knowledge of himself, man must first will and move towards self-inquiry and make himself an object of his study. Without willing, none of the things that ought to be done can be done. Unless one wills, one's moral powers remain idle, nowise leading their possessor to knowledge. The will activates them and renders them manifest. In man, the faculty of the will, strengthened by the faculty of reason and that of free choice and self-control, overcomes all obstacles and succeeds in everything: 'I will' becomes 'I can' in the man that acts with knowledge and freedom.

Man ought to will to know himself, to know God, and to understand the nature of things as they are in themselves, and thus become an image and likeness of God.

Those who know themselves are praised in adages as wise. The writer of the Proverbs, Solomon, says: "Those who know themselves are wise;" and he advises: "Know thyself and walk in the ways of your heart blameless."

The need of knowing ourselves has been taught by both religion and philosophy. Thales the Milesian held that the beginning of all the virtues is self-knowledge. The Oracle at Delphi called self-knowledge "the foremost and best part of true knowledge." Clearly, then, self-knowledge is the beginning of all virtue and wisdom. Now if the precept "Know thyself" is imposed upon us by our cognitive power as a Divine law written in our mind, we ought, as rational and morally free beings, to respect it and observe it.[16]

He who knows himself knows his duties towards himself, towards God, and towards his neighbor, and that piety, justice, truth and knowledge should be for him the touchstone on which he tests all his acts that have reference to God, to himself, and to his neighbor. . . . He who knows himself is never puffed up, never filled with pride, but first of all he knows his shortcomings and faults, always comparing himself with the ideal prototype, in the likeness of which he ought to develop himself, inasmuch as he sees how much he falls short of it.[17]

Man

Man is a composite being, made up of an earthly body and a celestial soul. . . . The soul is closely united with the body, yet wholly independent of it.

The existence and rationality of the soul are testified by consciousness, self-awareness, insight, self-observation, concepts, spiritual desires, love of the beautiful, the good, the true, the beneficial, the aversion towards evil, the distinction of good from evil, and every other manifest spiritual activity.[18]

* * *

Man is not only reason but also heart. The powers of these two centers, mutually assisting one another, render man perfect and teach him what he could never learn through reason alone. If reason teaches about the natural world, the heart teaches us about the supernatural world. . . . Man is perfect when he has developed both his heart and his intellect. Now the heart is developed through revealed religion.[19]

* * *

Man was created a religious and social being;

both of these are essential characteristics of man and virtues innate in him. His sociability is shown to be absolutely necessary for his preservation, development and advancement, while his religiousness is a consequence of his rationality and his power of free choice and self-control.[20]

Without religion man is an incomprehensible mystery. His existence on earth as a rational being having the power of free choice and self-ruling is, without religion, devoid or sufficient reason, because reason without moral principles is a means of corruption of the divine image, a destroyer of the beautiful, the good, and the true. Without religion, man becomes an antagonizing power, opposing the will of God and combating the laws in accordance with which the universe is led to a preordained goal.[21]

Immortality of the Soul

The rational soul of man has supernatural, infinite aspirations. If the rational soul were dependent upon the body and died together with the body, it should necessarily submit to the body and follow it in all its appetites. Independence would have been contrary both to the laws of nature and to reason, because it disturbs the harmony between the body and the soul. As dependent upon the body it should submit to the body and follow it in all its appetites and desires, whereas, on the contrary, the soul masters the body, imposes its will upon the body. The soul subjugates and curbs the appetites and passions of the body, and directs them as it (the soul) wills. This phenomenon comes to the attention of every rational man; and whoever is conscious of his own rational soul is conscious of the soul's mastery over the body.

The mastery of the soul over the body is proved by the obedience of the body when it is being led with self-denial to sacrifice for the sake of the abstract ideas of the soul. The domination by the soul for the prevalence of its principles, ideas, and views would have been entirely incomprehensible if the soul died together with the body. But a mortal soul would never have risen to such a height, would never have condemned itself to death along with the body for the prevalence of abstract ideas that lacked meaning, since no noble idea, no noble and courageous thought has any meaning for a mortal soul.

A soul, therefore, which is capable of such things, must be immortal.[22]

Life After Death

The Teachers of the Eastern Orthodox Church, having Holy Scripture as their foundation, teach that those who die in the Lord go to a place of rest, according to the statement in the Apocalypse: "Blessed are the dead who die in the Lord from henceforth. Yea, saith the Spirit, that they may rest from their labors; and their works do follow them" (Rev. 14:13). This place of rest is viewed as the spiritual Paradise, where the souls of those who have died in the Lord, the souls of the righteous, enjoy the blessings of rest, while awaiting the day of rewarding and the prize of the high calling of God in Christ Jesus. . . .

About the sinners, they teach that their souls go down to Hades, where there is suffering, sorrow, and groaning, awaiting the dreadful day of the Judgment.

The Fathers of the Orthodox Church do not admit the existence of another place, intermediate between Paradise and Hades, as such a place is not mentioned in Holy Scripture.[23]

After death, the souls are in a state which does not have complete retribution, either for virtue or for vice. This state will continue until the Great Judgment, which will take place after the Second Coming (*Parousia*) of Christ. In this state, the souls of the righteous have a foretaste of the blessedness prepared for them, while the sinners experience to a certain extent the eternal and complete suffering that awaits them. According to Origen, in this state the souls are purified through a certain spiritual fire. This teaching about a purifying fire was spread by Augustine in the Western Church, where it was elevated to the status of a dogma of faith by Gregory the Great. But in the Eastern Church the belief in a purgatorial fire was never recognized as sound.[24]

* * *

The Partial Judgment, to which all men are subjected after death, is by no means complete and final, wherefore it naturally follows that they await another, complete and final judgment. During the Partial Judgment, only the soul of man receives its retribution, not the body as well, even though the latter shared with the soul its deeds, good or evil. After the Partial Judgment, the righteous in Heaven and the sinners in Hades have only a foretaste of the blessedness or punishments which they deserve. Finally, after this Partial Judgment some of the sinners will be relieved of the burden of the punishment and will be completely delivered from sufferings of Hades, not through their own action, but through the prayers of the Church.[25]

*   *   *

Their separation from God is the most painful suffering which sinners experience, because they are deprived of participation in the Kingdom of Heaven, the blessedness of the righteous, and cast in a state of darkness. Also, they experience remorse of conscience, which, being aroused against their sins, torments them unceasingly, like the worm that does not die: "Where their worm dieth not, and the fire is not quenched."[26] And they are in the company of evil spirits. . . . It must be stated that the sufferings of the sinners in Hades are certainly not the same for all, but proportionate to the sins of each, as is indicated in Luke 12: 47-48.[27]

*   *   *

After the end of the General Judgment, the Righteous Judge will declare the decision both to the righteous and to the sinners. To the righteous He will say: "Come, ye blessed of my Father, inherit the Kingdom prepared for you from the foundation of the world;"[28] while to the sinners He will say: "Depart from me, ye cursed, into everlasting fire, prepared for the devil and his angels."[29] And these will go away to eternal hell, while the righteous will go to eternal life. This retribution after the General Judgment will be complete, final, and definitive. It will be complete, because it is not the soul alone, as at the **Partial** Judgment of man after death, but the soul together with the body, that will receive what is deserved. It will be final, because it will be enduring and not temporary like that at **Partial** Judgment. And it will be definitive, because both for the righteous and for the sinners it will be unalterable and eternal.[30]

Saints

Our Church honors saints not as gods, but as faithful servants, as holy men and friends of God. It extols the struggles they engaged in and the deeds they performed for the glory of God with the action of His grace, in such a way that all the honor that the Church gives them refers to the Supreme Being, Who has viewed their life on earth with gratification. The Church honors them by commemorating them annually through public celebrations and through the erection of churches in honor of their name.[31]

The holy men of God, who were magnified on earth by the Lord, have been honored by God's

holy Church from the very time it was founded
by the Savior Christ.[32]

The honor given to saints is dictated by lofty
religious feeling and the divine zeal of a heart that
is faithful to God and loves Him, and is a manifestation of the divine aspiration that fills it to glorify God Who glorifies His Church Militant. The
honor given to saints is an expression of the love
of the faithful towards them for their sublime
virtues and great struggles, whereby they received
the unwithering crown of glory. The honor given
to saints is a confirmation of the eros that is burning in our soul for rising to the height of their
virtues, which abide as an eternal example for us.
The honor given to saints is a moral obligation
towards them for their manifold benefactions to
us. . . . Failure to give due honor and reverence
to the saints of God is impiety, ingratitude, indifference, and lack of aspiration for self-perfection
in virtue.[33]

*   *   *

The Church invokes the saints in its prayers as
intercessors with God, and also honors their relics
and everything that belonged to them, as well as
icons depicting them.[34]

*   *   *

From the Orthodox standpoint, the concept of the Church contains in itself the dogma of the intercession of the saints, which was universal in the Church of the first centuries, was regarded from the beginning as an undoubted truth, and has been held as such throughout the centuries.[35]

In invoking the intercession of the saints, the Church believes that the saints, who interceded with the Lord for the peace of the world and for the stability of the holy churches of Christ while living, do not cease doing this in Christ's heavenly, Triumphant Church, and listen to our entreaties in which we invoke them, and pray to the Lord, and become bearers of the grace and mercy of the Lord.[36]

Repentance

Two factors are involved in man's salvation: the grace of God and the will of man. Both must work together, if salvation is to be attained. . . .[37]

Grace does not save without the consent of man. . . . One must return to his Lord God, repent for one's sins. . . . Grace does not descend upon one who is enslaved to sin, for there is no

communion between light and darkness. In order
to save man, grace must find him pure, for it is not
merely a question of being delivered from bondage to the devil, but also of reconciliation with
God, of communion with Him, of man's deification. For this reason the baptism of repentance
(*metanoia*) is needed, purity of life, moral preparation. . . . There is need of man's voluntary consent, his spontaneous movement towards God, his
will to return to God, his entry into the bath of
regeneration, in order to be cleansed, sanctified,
and saved.[38]

Repentance is a Mysterion through which he
who repents for his sins confesses before a Spiritual Father who has been appointed by the
Church and has received the authority to forgive
sins, and receives from this Spiritual Father the
remission of his sins and is reconciled with the
Deity, against Whom he sinned.

Repentance is a bath that cleanses one of his
own sins. It is a return from a state contrary to
nature to a state in accordance with nature, from
the devil to God, through spiritual striving and
painful efforts. It is a voluntary return from of-
fences to the good that is opposed to them.[39]

Repentance signifies regret, change of mind. The distinguishing marks of repentance are contrition, tears, aversion towards sin, and love of the good.[40]

The grace of God abandons the unrepentant man. . . . An example of abandonment by God testified by Scripture is Sedecias, king of Judaia. He was abandoned by God and was destroyed together with his kingdom, even though he sought the grace of God through the Prophet Jeremiah. It is truly dreadful, yet also just. It is just that he who abandons God should be abandoned by Him; just that he who repels Divine grace, which invites Him, should be repelled; just that God should turn His face away from one who turns away from Him.[41]

Virtue

We ought to do everything we can for the acquisition of virtue and moral wisdom (*phronesis*), for the prize is beautiful and the hope great.[42]

* * *

The path of virtue is a path of effort and toil: "Strait is the gate, and narrow is the way, which leadeth unto life, and few there be that find it;"[43]

whereas the gate of vice is wide and the way spacious, but lead to perdition.[44]

*   *   *

Virtue is the fulfillment of the Law of God. Basil the Great says: "Virtue is the avoidance of evil and the doing of good." He who partakes of true virtue partakes of nothing other than God, for God is complete virtue. Basil says: "Of all our possessions, virtue is the only one which cannot be taken away, abiding with us both in this life and after death."[45]

Faith, hope, and love were the common commandments which Jesus taught men. They are the fundamental virtues of Christianity, revealed to the world by God. *Faith* is the foremost source of virtue and power. *Hope* is consolation, relief, solace of those in sorrow, saving them from the abyss of despair, and relieving the heavy-laden soul from the weight of the injustices of the world and of heavy and violent misfortune: "Come unto me, all ye that labor and are heavy-laden, and I will give you rest."[46] *Love* is the bond that unites society, and the fraternization of the whole of mankind. It is the basis of the happiness of men, and the foundation of all the virtues. It is the ladder that elevates man to perfection, rendering him a true image and likeness of God.[47]

* * *

Love of God is knowledge of God, for one who loves, loves what one has come to know, and it is impossible for one to love what is unknown. . . . Love of God expresses the yearning to be united with God as the supreme good.[78]

Spiritual Training

Spiritual training (*pneumatike gymnasia*) is askesis for piety. It is most valuable, "having promise for the life that now is, and for that which is to come."[79] The efforts made for the sake of piety bring spiritual gladness.

Theophylaktos[50] says: "Train yourself for piety, that is, for pure faith and the right life. Training, then, and continual efforts are necessary; for he who trains exercises until he perspires, even when there is no contest."

Fasting, hardship, and askesis in general are spiritual training.

Training accustoms one to be lenient, temperate, capable of controlling his anger, subduing his desires, doing works of charity, showing love for his fellow men, practicing every virtue. Training is virtuous askesis, rendering one's way of life admirable.

Askesis is practice, meditation, training, self-control, love of labor.[51]

*   *   *

When you see great spiritual askesis know that there is great moral virtue, which sustains bodily askesis. For we must realize well that the strength of the soul strengthens and supports the body in its struggles. Without strength of the soul great askesis is impossible; and if a rash person should undertake great askesis before he strengthens his soul through the moral virtues, such a person will go astray and fall.[52]

Fasting

Fasting is an ordinance of the Church, obliging the Christian to observe it on specific days. Concerning fasting, our Savior teaches: "When thou fastest, anoint thine head, and wash thy face; that thou appear not unto men to fast, but unto thy Father Who is in secret: and thy Father, Who seeth in secret, shall reward thee openly."[53] From what the Savior teaches we learn (a) that fasting is pleasing to God, and (b) that he who fasts for the uplifting of his mind and heart towards God shall be rewarded by God, Who is a most liberal bestower of Divine gifts, for his devotion.

Fasting was observed by the holy Apostles. In the Acts of the Apostles we read: "As they ministered to the Lord, and fasted, the Holy Spirit said. . . . "[54] And immediately after this, we read: "When they had fasted and prayed, and laid their hands on them, they sent them away."[55] And in another chapter we read: "And when they had ordained for them elders in every church, and had prayed with fasting, they commended them to the Lord."[56]

In the New Testament fasting is recommended as a means of preparing the mind and the heart for divine worship, for long prayer, for rising from the earthly, and for spiritualization.

Fasting is enjoined in the Old Testament also, and was practiced by the Jews.[57]

The purpose of fasting is chiefly spiritual: to provide an opportunity and preparation for the spiritual works of prayer and meditation on the Divine through the complete abstinence from food, or the eating of uncooked food[58] or frugal fare. However, fasting is no less valuable for physical health, since self-control and simplicity of life are necessary conditions of health and longevity, as dietetics tells us.[59]

Inner Attention

Attention is the first teacher of truth and consequently absolutely necessary. Attention rouses the soul to study itself and its longings, to learn their true character and repulse those that are unholy. Attention is the guardian angel of the intellect, always counseling it this: be attentive. Attention awakens the soul, rouses it from sleep. . . . Attention examines every thought, every desire, every memory. Thoughts, desires, and memories are engendered by various causes, and often appear masked and with a splendid garb, in order to deceive the inattentive intellect and enter into the soul and dominate it. Only attention can reveal their hidden form. Often their dissimulation is so perfect that the discernment of their true nature is very difficult and requires the greatest attention. One must remember the saving words of the Lord: "Be wakeful and pray that ye enter not into temptation."[60] He who is wakeful does not enter into temptation, because he is vigilant and attentive.[61]

*   *   *

Attention directs the thoughts. Attention shows what ought to be done. Attention leads to virtue. Attention guards character. Attention is the only safe guide in life. Attention leads to blessedness. Lack of attention leads to unhappiness. Observe yourself, and you shall not fail in life. . . . Paul says: "See that ye walk circumspectly, not as fools, but as wise, redeeming the time, because the days are evil."[62]

Prayer

True prayer is undistracted, prolonged, performed with a contrite heart and an alert intellect. The vehicle of prayer is everywhere humility, and prayer is a manifestation of humility. For being conscious of our own weakness, we invoke the power of God.

Prayer unites one with God, being a divine conversation and spiritual communion with the Being that is most beautiful and highest.

Prayer is a forgetting of earthly things, an ascent to heaven. Through prayer we flee to God.

Prayer is truly a heavenly armor, and it alone

can keep safe those who have dedicated themselves to God. Prayer is the common medicine for purifying ourselves from the passions, for hindering sin and curing our faults. Prayer is an inexhaustible treasure, an unruffled harbor, the foundation of serenity, the root and mother of myriads of blessings.[63]

*   *   *

Every Christian should know that unless one lifts his mind and heart towards God through Christian — not Pharisaic — fasting and through prayer, he cannot attain a profound consciousness of his sinful state and earnestly seek the forgiveness of his sins. It should be realized that we know our sins only to the extent that we are illumined from Above, and that we are illumined from Above in proportion as our mind and heart rise up to God; and that we rise in proportion as the soul becomes lighter through fasting and prayer. Prayer and fasting — Christian fasting — serve as means of self-study, of discernment of our true moral state, of an accurate estimation of our sins, and of a knowledge of their true character. Without fasting and prayer we lack the means of acquiring this knowledge, and we cannot have a true picture of our sins, a perfect awareness of them and contrition of the heart, and hence true and fruitful confession. Inasmuch, then, as Christian fasting and prayer are the only way of preparation for true confession, we ought to observe diligently these decrees of the Church, in order not to fail in our aim, but succeed in attaining the supreme good towards which we aspire.[64]

Holy Communion

The Mysterion of the Divine Eucharist that has been handed down by the Lord is the highest of all the Mysteria; it is the most wondrous of all the miracles which the power of God has performed; it is the highest which the wisdom of God has conceived; it is the most precious of all the gifts which the love of God has bestowed upon men. For all the other miracles result through a transcendence of certain laws of Nature, but the Mysterion of the Divine Eucharist transcends all these laws. Hence it may justly be called, and be viewed as, the miracle of miracles and the Mysterion of Mysteria.[65]

*   *   *

To those who receive Holy Communion worthily, it offers not only salvation, but also a great number of other gifts, through which man is rendered an image and likeness of God. Through Divine Communion we are united with God and enter into relation and contact with Him. Through such union we receive the gifts of the Holy Spirit: love, joy, peace, forbearance, goodness, faith, meekness, self-control, and so many other virtues. The eyes of our soul are opened, the mind is illumined, and the heart is purified. Divine Communion cures the sick heart and body of those who approach it with faith. It often saves our life and rescues us from dangers, and effects many other marvelous things.[66]

*   *   *

O! How happy and blessed must be considered he who receives the Divine Mysteria worthily! Such a person comes out of the church wholly renewed, because the fire of the Deity, having entered into the soul of man through Divine Communion, burned up its sins, filled it with Divine grace, strengthened its powers, illumined the mind, and rendered the heart a tabernacle solely of the Holy Spirit.[67]

*   *   *

The Church pronounces aloud to those who are ready to partake of Holy Communion the following God-inspired words: "With fear of God,[68] faith and love draw near." And, indeed, who is it that is devoid of fear of God, faith, and love that can be regarded as worthy of Communion?[69]

Do you now want to become a partaker of the blessings conferred by Divine Communion? Do you want your salvation? Become a true Christian, have fear of God, faith in the Mysterion of Divine Communion, and love for God and for your neighbor.

Fasting, contrite church services, and abstinence from the causes of sin are so many means of repentance and preparation for Communion.[70]

Monasticism

The monastic way of life is self-denial and submission to Divine Law, non-possession-of-property, self-control, hardship, struggle together with unceasing prayer for the achievement of every virtue, and a patient striving for perfection. The divine John Climacos defines the monk as follows: "A monk is he who unceasingly constrains his nature, unfailingly guards his senses, keeps his body chaste, his mouth pure, and his mind illumined" (Discourse 1). And St. Isaac the Syrian says: "A monk is he who stays outside the world, always praying to God to attain to the future blessings. The wealth of the monk consists in contrite prayer of entreaty, and the joy which comes from faith and shines in the chambers of the mind."[71]

*   *   *

Every day I pronounce blessed those who have dedicated themselves to God, and who live and move in Him. What, indeed, is more precious than that way of life, what more glorious? It works beautifully the divine image and lends it its archetypal beauty. It leads to blessedness, it leads to spiritual philosophy, it reveals mysteries, it teaches truth, it causes the word of God to be fresh in the heart, it leads with sureness to the most longed for goal, it elevates man to Heaven. It renders breathing an unceasingly melody, it makes the whole of life harmonious, it unites man with the angels, it renders man Godlike, it leads him upward to the Divine, it unites him with God.[72]

Miracles

Miracles are not impossible from a logical standpoint, and right reason does not deny them. Natural laws do not have the claim to be the only ones, nor are they threatened with being overturned by the appearance of other laws, supernatural ones, which also are conducive to the development and furtherance of creation. . . . Miracles are a consequence of the Creator's love for his creatures.[73]

*   *   *

Miracles are effected through quite unusual laws, when man's imperfection requires Divine help. The appearance of new laws is not an overthrow of the established ones, because they are not introduced in order to replace them — for the latter remain unaffected after this — but in order to help suffering creation and in a way to aid the natural laws. The new laws would have been subversive only if they did not act like the rest of the laws to sustain, develop, and promote the created world, but did the opposite.[74]

NOTES

INTRODUCTORY

[1] *Hyperaspisis tes Aletheias kai Nike kata tou Diabolou*, 2nd ed., Hermoupolis, 1894; 3rd ed., Athens, 1966. (Year of 1st ed. not listed.)

[2] Statement taken from a copy, in my possession, of the original letter that is kept in the archives of Holy Trinity Convent in Aegina.

[3] Archimandrite Titos Matthaiakis, *Ho Hosios Nektarios Kephalas* ("Saint Nectarios Kephalas"), Athens, 1955, p. 214.

[4] After this had been written, and this chapter had been printed, a number of other pamphlets published at that time in Athens came to my attention. They have been listed under the heading "Pamphlets" in the chapter "Works of the Saint."

[5] *Peri Pisteos.*

[6] *Peri Exomologeseos.*

[7] *Peri tes Theias Eucharistias*, p. 3.

[8] Warden, representative.

[9] Pentapolis, in older times a glorious Metropolis of Egypt, was no longer extant. Hence, in being thus ordained, he was to serve as Metropolitan of Cairo.

[10] See the letter of the Saint in Matthaiakis, *op. cit.*, p. 240. Cf. Theocletos Dionysiatis, *Ho Hagios Nektarios Aigines*, Thessaloniki, 1979, p. 31.

[11] See Matthaiakis, *op. cit.*, p. 35.

[12] *Deka Ekklesiastikoi logoi dia ten Megalen Tessarakosten.* This book I have not been able to find, but it is mentioned by his biographers.

[13] Matthaiakis, *op. cit.* 102.

[14] *Dyo Logoi Ekklesiastikoi.*

[15] *Ibid.*, p. 4.

[16] *Ibid.*, p. 6.

[17] *Peri ton Hieron Synodon, kai Idios peri tes Spoudaiotetos ton Dyo Proton Oikoumenikon Synodon.*

[18] *Logos Ekphonetheis en to Achillopouleio Parthenagogeio kata ten Heorten ton Trion Hierarchon.*

[19] *Schediasma peri Anexithreskeias.*

[20] P. 80.

[21] P. 81.

[22] *Christianike Ethike.*

[23] *Physike Theologia.*

[24] *Christianike Ethike tes Orthodoxou Anatolikes Ekklesias,* Athens, 1965, p. 5.

[25] *Peri ton Apotelesmaton tes Alethous kai Pseudous Morphoseos.*

[26] *Peri tes en to Kosmo Apokalypseos tou Theou.*

[27] *Ta Hiera Mnemosyna.*

[28] *Hai Oikoumenikai Synodoi tes tou Christou Ekklesias.*

[29] *Hypotyposis peri Anthropou.*

[30] P. 110.

[31] Matthaiakis, *op. cit.*, p. 103.

[32] *Peri tes Scheseos kai Diaphoras tes Psyches tou Anthropou kai tou Zoou.* This was published at Athens in 1885, under the title *Melete epi tes Psyches tou Anthropou kai tou Zoou* ("Study on the Soul of Man and of the Animal").

[33] Pp. 216-217.

[34] *Peri Epimeleias Psyches.*

[35] *Op. cit.*, 2nd ed., Athens, 1973, p. 110.

[36] *Ibid.*, pp. 23, 50.

[37] *Ibid.*, p. 16.

[38] Matthaiakis, *op. cit.*, p. 103.

[39] *Ibid.*, p. 44.

[40] *Ibid.*

[41] *Op. cit.*, pp. 139, 140.

[42] *Hieron kai Philosophikon Logion Thesaurisma*, Athens, 1894, p. iv.

[43] P. vi.

[44] Matthaiakis, *op. cit.*, pp. 50-51, 60.

[45] *Melete peri ton Hagion Eikonon*, 1902. See the chapter "Works of the Saint" in this book, under the heading "Articles."

[46] *Peri Horkou.* See the chapter and section mentioned in the preceding note.

[47] P. iv.

[48] *Ibid.*

[49] *Psalterion tou Prophetanaktos Dauid.* p. 6.

[50] P. 4.

[51] *Epikai kai Elegeiakai Gnomai ton Mikron Hellenon Poieton.*

[52] *Encheiridion Christianikes Ethikes.*

[53] *Christianike Ethike tes Orthodoxou Anatolikes Ekklesias.*

[54] *Mathema Poimantikes.*

[55] Pp. 125, 129. Cf. Plato, *Phaedo*, 89d.

[56] P. 129.

[57] Pp. 264-265.

[58] *Hiera Katechesis tes Anatolikes Orthodoxou Ekklesias.*

[59] Matthaiakis, *op. cit.*, pp. 103-104.

[60] *Christologia.*

[61] *Melete peri tes Athanasias tes Psyches kai peri ton Hieron Mnemosynon.*

[62] *Christology.*

[63] P. 5.

[64] *Ibid.*

[65] Pp. 50-53.

[66] *Study Concerning the Immortality of the Soul*, p. 65.

[67] *A Select Library of Nicene and Post-Nicene Fathers*, Second Series, ed. P. Schaff and H. Wace, Vol. 5, p. 431.

[68] *Euangelike Historia, di' Harmonias ton Keimenon ton Hieron Euangeliston Matthaiou, Markou, Louka kai Ioannou.*

[69] P. v.

[70] P. x.

[71] Matthaiakis, *op. cit.*, p. 104.

[72] *Proseuchetarion Katanyktikon.*

[73] *To Gnothi Sauton, etoi Meletai Threskeutikai kai Ethikai.*

[74] *Ho Hagios Nektarios Aigines, ho Thaumatourgos,* Thessaloniki, 1979, pp. 217-285. Matthaiakis has published, in his often referred to above work, forty-five letters to the nuns, among which are these thirty-five (pp. 193-252).

[75] *Melete peri tes Metros tou Kyriou, tes Hyperagias Theotokou kai Aeiparthenou Marias,* p. 3.

[76] P. 18.

[77] *Melete peri tou Mysteriou tes Theias Eucharistias.*

[78] *Ibid.,* pp. 23-24, 33.

[79] *Ibid.,* p. 33.

[80] *Holy Memorial Services,* pp. 44-45; *Study Concerning the Immortality of the Soul,* p. 105.

[81] *Theotokarion, etoi Proseuchetarion Mikron.*

[82] *Pandektes ton Theopneuston Hagion Graphon.*

[83] P. iv.

[84] P. v.

[85] *Ibid.*

[86] Matthaiakis, *op. cit.,* pp. 75-76.

[87] *Psalterion tou Prophetanaktos Dauid, Entetamenon eis Metra kata ten Toniken Basin, meta Hermeneutikon Semeioseon.*

[88] See my book *St. Nicodemos the Hagiorite* (Vol. 3 of *Modern Orthodox Saints*), 1974 and 1979, pp. 49-50.

[89] *The Psalter of the Prophet-king David,* p. 11.

[90] *Ibid.,* p. 13.

91 *Ibid.*, p. 10.

92 Matthaiakis, *op. cit.*, p. 60.

93 *Ibid.*, p. 61.

94 See e.g., his letter of June 20, 1914, in Matthaiakis, *op. cit.*, p. 268.

95 *Ibid.*, pp. 43-44.

96 P. 172.

97 *Triadikon, etoi Odai kai Hymnoi pros ton en Triadi Theon.* Athens, 1909.

98 *Kekragarion tou Theiou kai Hierou Augoustinou, Episkopou Hipponos, Entathen eis Metra kata ten Toniken Basin, ek tes Metaphraseos tou Eugeniou tou Boulgareos.*

99 *Melete Historike peri ton Aition tou Schismatos, peri tes Diaioniseos Autou, kai peri tou Dynatou e Adynatou tes Henoseos ton Dyo Ekklesion, tes Anatolikes kai tes Dytikes.*

100 Vol. 1, p. 3.

101 *Ibid.*, p. 5.

102 *Ibid.*, p. 8.

103 *Ibid.*, pp. 10-11.

104 *Ibid.*, p. 9.

105 *Meletai Dyo: A' Peri tes Mias Hagias Katholikes kai Apostolikes Ekklesias; B' Peri tes Hieras Paradoseos.*

106 P. 5.

107 P. 8. The quotation is from Matthew 23: 15.

108 *Ibid.*

109 *Op. cit.*, pp. 7-8.

110 *Ibid.*, p. 8.

[111] *Historike Melete peri tou Timiou Staurou.*

[112] P. 5.

[113] *Meletai peri ton Theion Mysterion.*

[114] P. 3.

[115] P. 4.

[116] *Melete peri Ekklesias.*

[117] *He Theia Leitourgia tou Hagiou and Endoxou Apostolou kai Euangelistou Markou.*

[118] *Historike Melete peri ton Diatetagmenon Nesteion.* For the place and date of publication of this and the preceding work see the chapter of this book entitled "Works of the Saint," under the heading "Articles."

[119] Matthaiakis, *op. cit.*, p. 106. The italics are mine.

[120] *Ibid.*, pp. 107-108. The italics are mine.

[121] See Vasilios Chr. Papanikolaou, *Ho Hagios Sabbas ho Neos ho en Kalymno* ("St. Savvas the New of Kalymnos"), 2nd ed., Kalymnos, 1979, pp. 23-24, 37, 56-58.

[122] *Ibid.*, pp. 25, 37-38.

[123] See e.g. Theodosios Papaconstantinou, *Biographike Skiagraphia kai Thaumata tou en Hosiois Patros hemon Nektariou.* Athens, 1952, pp. 14-18.

[124] *Biographia Metropolitou Pentapoleos en Makaria te Lexei Sebasmiotatou Nektariou,* in *Panegyrikon,* Volos, 1921, p. 66.

[125] See note 123 above.

[126] See its pamphlet: *1926-1956 — Trianta Chronia Ergasias kai Proergasias tou Syllogou.* Athens, 1956. This Society now has its office, a chapel, and a lecture room at 39 Isaurou Street, Athens, and has over 1000 members.

[127] The Act (*Praxis*) of recognition by the Oecumenical Patriarchate in its complete form is contained in Ioannes Gr. Timagenis, ed., *Hagios Nektarios, Episkopos Pentapoleos ho Thaumatourgos*, Athens, ca. 1967, pp. 57-59.

[128] Matthaiakis, *op. cit.*, pp. 129-130.

[129] *Ibid.*, p. 132.

[130] *Ibid.*, p. 100.

[131] *Ibid.*, p. 106.

[132] *Ibid.*, pp. 6, 11, 145.

[133] *Ouden Aniaton dia ton Hagion Nektarion.* Athens, ca. 1962.

[134] *Ho Hagios Nektarios.* Athens, 1968.

[135] *Ho Hagios Nektarios: Ho Hierarches, ho Logios, ho Asketes.* Athens, 1970.

[136] *Ho Hagios Nektarios Aigines, ho Thaumatourgos.* Thessaloniki, 1979.

[137] *Neon Chiakon Leimonarion.* Athens, 1968.

THE LIFE OF ST. NECTARIOS

By Joachim Spetsieris

[1] Archimandrite Joachim Spetsieris (c. 1858-1943), a native of the island of Kephallenia, led a hermit's life at the New Skete on the Holy Mountain of Athos from the age of eighteen to twenty-seven, and during the latter period of his life. In 1885, he went to Jerusalem. There he was ordained deacon and then priest, and studied at the School of the Holy Cross. In 1891, he was appointed parish priest at the Church of the Exarchate of the All-Holy Sepulchre in Athens. At this

time he began to study at the Rizarios Ecclesiastical School, which was placed under the direction of St. Nectarios in 1894, when Father Joachim was a third year student. After graduating from this school, he attended the School of Theology of the University of Athens, and received the Licentiate of Theology and the Doctor of Theology degree. Subsequently, he served as a preacher for a period of twenty-five years in various parts of Greece, including Messolonghi, Pyrgos, Corinth, Lamia, Amphissa, Ithaca, and Halkis. At first one of his teachers at the Rizarios School, St. Nectarios later became one of Father Spetsieris' close friends. Spetsieris authored 1) *The Hermitess Photini*, 2) *God*, 3) *Memoirs*, in three volumes, 4) *Festive Sermons*, 5) *Concerning Divine Communion*, 6) *Biographical Sketch of our Ever Memorable Holy Father and Hierarch Nectarios, Metropolitan of Pentapolis*, and other works. The first mentioned work is his most popular one, having gone through at least four editions. The text that follows is a slightly abridged translation which I have made of the last mentioned work, which was published at Athens in 1929, only nine years after the death of St. Nectarios. I have made certain corrections here and there on the basis of Archimandrite Titos' Matthaiakis' biography of the Saint, which is included in his book *Hosios Nectarios Kephalas* that was published in 1955 at Athens. Matthaiakis' had full access to the Saint's archives, and his biography is the most comprehensive and best documented one, though not written in the traditional style of Greek Orthodox lives of saints.

2 Euripides.

3 Heb. 13: 8.

4 Eph. 6: 4.

5 Rom. 8: 29.

6 A landed estate with a church, belonging to the All-Holy Sepulchre.

7 On November 7, 1876, at the age of thirty.

8 Psalm 144 (145): 19.

[9] He entered the University of Athens in 1882.

[10] On March 23, 1886.

[11] On January 15, 1889.

[12] The high esteem in which St. Nectarios was held by the people occasioned envy among those about the Patriarch, and they finally succeeded in arousing Patriarch Sophronios against him.

[13] That is, in liberated Greece. Mount Athos was at that time still under Turkish rule. Athos continued to have a strong attraction for the Saint long after this. He visited its monasteries in 1898, during the summer recess of the Rizarios School, of which he was then Director. (See T. Matthaiakis, *op. cit.*, p. 51.)

[14] The appointment was made on February 15, 1891, by the Ministry of Church Affairs, after it had been approved by the Holy Synod of the Church of Greece.

[15] On August 19, 1893.

[16] This school was established at Athens in 1844 for the training of priests. St. Nectarios was appointed its Director on March 8, 1894.

[17] "Regeneration." A religious periodical founded in 1887.

[18] His body was buried at the Convent of Holy Trinity which he established in Aegina.

[19] Psalm 144: 19 (Septuagint).

[20] According to Matthaiakis, the monastery was named *Zoodochos Pighi*, "Life-giving Fount" (*op. cit.*, pp. 6, 10).

[21] Spetsieris gives the year 1907. But this is not correct, for Nectarios served as Director of the Rizarios School until December, 1908. His letter of resignation, which appears in the already mentioned work of Matthaiakis (p. 41), was written on December 7, 1908.

[22] A coenobitic monastery is one which is governed by an abbot or abbess, and in which all property is held in common and the meals are partaken by all together in the refectory. A blind nun, named Xenia, served as the first abbess, from 1904 to 1923, when she died.

[23] Matt. 5: 15.

[24] Besides serving as priest of the convent and as the Spiritual Father of the nuns, St. Nectarios "occupied himself sometimes with manual work of a heavy nature, such as tilling the gardens and farms, watering them with water that he carried from a long distance, opening water-courses and sewers, carrying large stones on his shoulders for the construction of cells for the convent, and repairing the shoes of the nuns" (Matthaiakis, *op. cit.*, p. 60).

[25] Archimandrite Amphilochios Makris (of the Monastery of St. John the Theologian in Patmos), who knew St. Nectarios personally, having associated with him from 1914 to the time of his death, remarks: "He was a man of prayer, and had one thought, how to create centers of prayer. He spoke of mental prayer because he had cultivated this higher mode of prayer in himself" (Matthaiakis, *op. cit.*, p. 132).

[26] Spetsieris says that the Saint suffered for "five whole months from cystitis;" Theodosios Papaconstantinou, that he suffered from "cystitis for fifteen whole months" (*Biographical Sketch*, Athens, 1952, 1963, p. 22). Matthaiakis, having more accurate information at his disposal, says that he suffered from *prostatitis* "for a year and a half" (*op. cit.*, p. 62.).

[27] The body was again found whole and incorrupt. It remained in such a state until a few years prior to September 2, 1953, when the actual removal of the relics took place. (See Matthaiakis, *op. cit.*, pp. 9, 11, 82.)

[28] After the removal of the remains of the Saint from the tomb, they were found to emit an ineffable fragrance stronger than before. (Matthaiakis, *op. cit.*, pp. 11, 62).

SOME MIRACLES OF THE SAINT

[1] *Ouden Aniaton dia ton Hagion Nektarion*, Athens, year not listed.

[2] *Ho Hagios Nektarios*, Athens, 1970.

[3] Dem. Panagopoulos, *op. cit.*, 6th edition, pp. 50-51. This miracle brings to mind a similar one attributed to the Apostle Paul in the Acts of the Apostles: "And God wrought extraordinary miracles by the hands of Paul, so that from his body were brought to the sick handkerchiefs or aprons, and the diseases departed from them" (19: 11-12). St. Arsenios of Paros is credited with the performance of a similar miracle. See my book *St. Arsenios of Paros* (Vol. 6 of *Modern Orthodox Saints*), Belmont, 1978, pp. 86-87.

[4] Dem. Panagopoulos, *op. cit.*, p. 267.

[5] *Ibid.*, pp. 95-96.

[6] *Ibid.*, pp. 108-110.

[7] *Ibid.*, pp. 212-213.

[8] *Ibid.*, pp. 165-166.

[9] *Op. cit.*, 7th edition, p. 248.

ON GOD

[1] *Concerning God's Revelation in the World*, pp. vi-vii.

[2] *Ibid.*, p. 36.

[3] *Ibid.*, p. 37.

[4] *Ibid.*

[5] Constantine Cavarnos, *Anchored in God*, 1959, 1975, pp. 189-190.

[6] *Concerning God's Revelation in the World*, p. 38.

[7] *Ibid.*, p. 37.

[8] *Ibid.*, p. 56.

[9] *Ibid.*

[10] *Ibid.*, p. 38.

[11] *Ibid.*, p. 39.

[12] *Ibid.*

[13] *Ibid.*

[14] *Ibid.*

[15] *Know Thyself*, p. 175.

[16] *Ibid.*, p. 193.

[17] *Ibid.*

[18] *Ibid.*

[19] *Op. cit.*, p. 221,

[20] *Christology*, Athens, 1901, p. 7.

[21] *Ibid.*, pp. 8-9.

[22] *Know Thyself*, p. 183.

[23] *Treasury of Sacred and Philosophical Sayings*, Vol. 1, Athens, 1895, p. 12, Vol. 2, 1896, p. 42.

[24] *The Oecumenical Synods of the Church of Christ*, pp. 221-222.

[25] *Ibid.*, p. 222.

[26] *Ibid.*

[27] *Ibid.*, pp. 222-223.

[28] *Ibid.*, p. 223.

[29] *Ibid.*

[30] *Ibid.*

[31] *Historical Study Concerning the Causes of the Schism,* p. 249.

[32] *Ibid.*

[33] *Sacred Catechism of the Eastern Orthodox Church,* p. 21.

[34] *Ibid.*

[35] *Ibid.*, p. 22.

[36] *Ibid.*

[37] *Ibid.*

[38] *Ibid.*, pp. 23-27.

[39] *Ibid.*, pp. 27-30.

[40] *Ibid.*, p. 77.

[41] *Ibid.*, pp. 74-75.

[42] *Ibid.*, p. 75.

[43] *Ibid.*

[44] *Ibid.*, p. 76.

[45] *Ibid.*

SELECTED PASSAGES FROM
THE WRITINGS OF THE SAINT

[1] *The Oecumenical Synods of the Church of Christ,* Athens, 1892, p. 170.

[2] *Ibid.*, p. 42.

[3] *Know Thyself*, 2nd ed., Athens, 1962, p. 193.

[4] *Ibid.*, pp. 193-194.

[5] *Ibid.*, p. 193.

[6] Titos Matthaiakis, *Saint Nectarios Kephalas*, Athens, 1955, p. 216.

[7] *Ibid.*, p. 221.

[8] *Two Studies*, Athens, 1913, p. 9.

[9] *Ibid.*, p. 10.

[10] *Ibid.*, p. 21.

[11] *Ibid.*, p. 34.

[12] *Ibid.*, p. 83.

[13] *Sermon, on the First Sunday of the Fasts, Concerning Faith*, Athens, 1885, p. 4.

[14] *Ibid.*, pp. 4-5.

[15] *Know Thyself*, p. 5.

[16] *Ibid.*, pp. 5-6. The first of Solomon's sayings is from Proverbs 13: 10; the second, from Ecclesiastes 11: 9 (Sept.).

[17] *Concerning the Results of True and Pseudo Education*, Athens, 1894, pp. 8, 13.

[18] *Sketch Concerning Man*, Athens, 1895, pp. 173, 32.

[19] *The Oecumenical Synods*, p. 43, *Concerning God's Revelation in the World*, Athens, 1892, p. 43.

[20] *Course in Pastoral Theology*, Athens, 1898, p. v.

[21] *Ibid.*, p. vi.

[22] *Study Concerning the Immortality of the Soul and*

Holy Memorial Services, Athens, 1901, pp. 37-38. In this book St. Nectarios gives twenty proofs of immortality. Eighteen of these appear in English translation in my book *Modern Greek Philosophers on the Human Soul*, Belmont, Mass., 1967, pp. 61-86.

[23] *Ibid.*, p. 151.

[24] *Ibid.*, p. 170.

[25] *Ibid.*, p. 173.

[26] Mark 9: 44.

[27] *Study Concerning the Immortality of the Soul*, p. 186.

[28] Matt. 25: 34.

[29] Matt. 25: 41.

[30] *Study Concerning the Immortality of the Soul*, pp. 187-188.

[31] *Study Concerning the Saints of God*, Athens, 1904, p. 3.

[32] *Ibid.*, pp. 3-4.

[33] *Ibid.*, p. 4.

[34] *Ibid.*, p. 3.

[35] *Ibid.*, p. 12.

[36] *Ibid.*, p. 18.

[37] *Study Concerning the Mysterion of the Divine Eucharist*, Athens, 1904, p. 24.

[38] *Studies Concerning the Divine Mysteria*, Athens, 1915, pp. 66-67.

[39] *Ibid.*, p. 67.

[40] *Ibid.*, pp. 67-68.

[41] *Ibid.*, pp. 79, 80.

[42] *Study Concerning the Results of True and Pseudo Education*, p. 16. This is a statement taken from Plato's *Phaedo* (114c). St. Nectarios quotes it in concluding the first chapter.

[43] Matt. 7: 14.

[44] *Study Concerning the Results of True and Pseudo Education*, p. 6.

[45] *Know Thyself*, p. 138.

[46] Matt. 11: 28.

[47] *Concerning God's Revelation in the World*, pp. 84-85.

[48] *Sacred Catechism of the Eastern Orthodox Church*, Athens, 1899, p. 145.

[49] 1 Tim. 4: 8.

[50] Archbishop of Bulgaria (?1030-?1126) and an important Church writer.

[51] *Know Thyself*, pp. 169-170.

[52] Titos Matthaiakis, *op. cit.*, p. 231.

[53] Matt. 6: 17-18.

[54] Acts 13: 2.

[55] Acts 13: 3.

[56] Acts 14: 23.

[57] *Historical Study Concerning the Ordained Fasts*, Athens, 1956, p. 5.

[58] *Xerophagia*, literally "eating dry food."

[59] *Historical Study Concerning the Ordained Fasts*, p. 14.

[60] Matt. 26: 41.

[61] *Know Thyself*, pp. 190-191.

[62] *Ibid.*, p. 168. The quotation is from Ephesians 5:15-16.

[63] *Ibid.*, p. 44.

[64] *Study Concerning the Immortality of the Soul*, pp. 224-225.

[65] *Study Concerning the Mysterion of the Divine Eucharist*, p. 19.

[66] *Ibid.*, pp. 33-34.

[67] *Ibid.*, p. 23.

[68] That is, with deep humility, reverence, awe.

[69] *Study Concerning the Mysterion of the Divine Eucharist*, p. 31.

[70] *Ibid.*, pp. 34-35.

[71] *Know Thyself*, p. 172.

[72] Titos Matthaiakis, *op. cit.*, p. 261.

[73] *Concerning God's Revelation in the World*, pp. 22.

[74] *Ibid.*, pp. 37-38.

BIBLIOGRAPHY

Avimelech, Monk, of Crete, *Biographia Metro-politou Pentapoleos en Makaria te Lexei Se-basmiotatou Nektariou* ("Biography of the Metropolitan of Pentapolis Nectarios, on the Occasion of his Blessed Repose"), in *Pane-gyrikon*, Volos, 1921.

Cavarnos, Constantine, *Modern Greek Philoso-phers on the Human Soul*. Belmont, Massachu-setts, 1967. (Pp. 59-86 contain, abridged, in translation, 18 arguments of St. Nectarios for the immortality of the soul.)

El-Makari, Michael, *Ho Pentapoleos Nektarios* ("Nectarios, Metropolitan of Pentapolis"), in *Ekthesis peri ton kata ten Rizareion Scholen* ("An Account of Matters Pertaining to the Rizarios School"), Athens, 1901.

206

Gerasimos Micragiannanitis, Monk, *Ho Hagios Nektarios ho Thaumatourgos* ("Saint Nectarios the Miracle-Worker"). Comprises the Akolouthia, the Oikoi, and the Life of the Saint. Siderokastron, 1966. Reprinted in *Neon Chiakon Leimonarion* ("New Chian Leimonarion"), Athens, 1968, pp. 62-90.

Kostourakis, K. A., *Bios, Politeia, kai Thaumata tou Hagiou Nektariou Aigines* ("The Life Conduct, and Miracles of Saint Nectarios of Aegina"). Athens, 1963; Hania, Crete, 1965.

Matthaiakis Titos, Archimandrite, *Ho Hosios Nektarios Kephalas* ("Saint Nectarios Kephalas"). Athens, 1955.

Matthaiakis, Titos, Archimandrite, *Ho Hosios Nektarios Pentapoleos*: *Bios kai Akolouthia* ("Saint Nectarios, Metropolitan of Pentapolis: His Life and Akolouthia"). Athens, 1965.

Nectarios Kephalas, St., Works. (See the chapter: "Works of the Saint," in this book.)

Panagopoulos, Demetrios, *Ouden Aniaton dia ton Hagion Nektarion* ("Nothing is Incurable for Saint Nectarios"). Athens, 6th and 7th editions. (The year of publication is not listed, but from the dates of some of the miracles described it may be inferred that the 6th edition was published about 1965, and the 7th about 1971.)

Papaconstantinou, Theodosios, Archimandrite, *Akolouthia, Bios, kai Thaumata tou en Hosiois Patros hemon Nektariou, Metropolitou Pentapoleos* ("Akolouthia, Life, and Miracles of Our Holy Father Nectarios, Metropolitan of Pentapolis") . Athens, 1937.

Papaconstantinou, Theodosios, Archimandrite, *Biographike Skiagraphia kai Thaumata tou en Hosiois Aeimnestou Patros hemon kai Poimenarchou Nektariou, Metropolitou Pentapoleos* ("Biographical Sketch and Miracles of Our Ever Memorable Father and Prelate Saint Nectarios, Metropolitan of Pentapolis") . Athens, 1952; 2nd edition, 1963.

Papanikolaou, Vasilios Chr., *Ho Hagios Sabbas ho Neos ho en Kalymno* ("Saint Savvas the New of Kalymnos") . Kalymnos, 1975; 2nd edition, 1979.

Spetsieris, Joachim, Archimandrite, *Biographike Skiagraphia tou en Hosiois Aeimnestou Patros hemon kai Poimenarchou Nektariou, Metropolitou Pentapoleos* ("Biographical Sketch of

Our Ever Memorable Father Saint Nectarios,
Metropolitan of Pentapolis"). Athens, 1929.

Theocletos Dionysiatis, Monk, *Ho Hagios Nektarios Aigines, ho Thaumatourgos* ("Saint Nectarios of Aegina, the Miracle-Worker"). Thessaloniki, 1979.

Theodoretos, Monk of Athos, *Ho Hagios Nektarios: Ho Hierarches, ho Logios, ho Asketes* ("Saint Nectarios: The Hierarch, the Scholar, the Ascetic"). Athens, 1970.

Timagenis, Ioannes Gr., *Hagios Nektarios, Episkopos Pentapoleos, ho Thaumatourgos: Bios kai Politeia — Thaumata — Asmatike Akolouthia — Parakletikos Kanon* ("Saint Nectarios, Bishop of Pentapolis, the Miracle-Worker: His Life and Conduct — Miracles — Akolouthia, consisting of hymns designed to be chanted — Canon of Entreaty"). Athens, 1968.

Timotheos, Metropolitan of Gortyne and Arcadia, *Ho Hagios Nektarios* ("Saint Nectarios"). Moires, Crete, 1966.

Trianta Chronia Ergasias kai Proergasias tou Syllogou, 1926-1956 ("Thirty Years of Work and Preliminary Work, 1926-1956"). Athens, 1956. A pamphlet describing the establishment and activities of the Orthodox Christian Society *Ho Hagios Pentapoleos Nektarios,* "Saint Nectarios, Metropolitan of Pentapolis."

Varnavas, Metropolitan of Kitrous, *Nektarios ho Kephalas* ("Nectarios Kephalas"), in *Threskeutike kai Ethike Enkyklopaideia* ("Religious and Ethical Encyclopedia"), Vol. 9, Athens, 1966, cols. 397-399.

Vasilopoulos, Haralampos, Archimandrite, *Ho Hagios Nektarios* ("Saint Nectarios"). Athens, 1968. Reprinted seven times since then.

INDEX

Acts of the Apostles, Interpretation of, 128
Alexandria, 14-15, 17, 19, 21, 22, 23, 91-93, 95, 100
Alivizatos, Amilkas, 75
America, 83, 105
Amphilochios Makris, 79, 80, 198
Angels, 60, 156, 158, 186
anthropology, Christian, 28
Antiochos, monk, 56, 57, 122
Apologists, 73
Apostles, 27, 42, 43, 68, 69, 72, 126, 150, 158-160, 179
Apostolic Fathers, 73
aretology, 49
Aristotle, 26, 34, 36, 50
Arius, 145
Arsenios of Paros, St., 199
Arsenios the Great, St., 100
ascetic, 32, 34, 60-61, 81, 82, 84, 209
askesis, 82, 177-178
Athens, 14-15, 17, 25, 30-32, 61, 75, 81, 83, 91, 92, 95, 100
Athos, Mount, 23-24, 65-66, 75, 78, 79, 83, 84, 92, 133-134,
    195, 197, 209
Augustine, St., 38, 65, 99, 123, 169
Avimelech, monk, 77, 206